Torah Conversations with Nechama Leibowitz

Torah Conversations with Nechama Leibowitz

Rabbi Benjamin S. Yasgur

URIM PUBLICATIONS
Jerusalem • New York

Torah Conversations with Nechama Leibowitz
by Benjamin S. Yasgur

Copyright © 2013 by Benjamin S. Yasgur

Cover image: Nechama Leibowitz in her apartment in
front of a living room wall lined with extra copies of her
thirty year collection of weekly gilyonot, study sheets.
Professor Leibowitz used these gilyonot during classes and
presentations. Photo was taken by the author in Kislev 5751/
December 1990.

Book design by Ariel Walden

Printed in Israel.
ISBN-13: 978-965-524-069-6

Urim Publications
P.O. Box 52287, Jerusalem 91521 Israel

Lambda Publishers Inc.
527 Empire Blvd., Brooklyn, New York 11225 U.S.A.
Tel: 718-972-5449 Fax: 718-972-6307, mh@ejudaica.com

www.UrimPublications.com

This book is dedicated to the memory of my mother *z"l*

פראדל רחל בת מרדכי יוסף

FLORENCE FISHMAN YASGUR

whose love, patience and commitment to Judaism and
learning continue to inspire and guide me.

With appreciation and admiration to my wife, BARBARA,
for her love, encouragement and vision.

In honor of our CHILDREN, their SPOUSES and
our GRANDCHILDREN.

May you, and all other readers of this volume,
merit the blessing extended to me by NECHAMA LEIBOWITZ:

תזכו ללמוד תורה בשמחה

May you merit to study Torah in happiness.

CONTENTS

Of the seminal events in my life, studying with the late Professor Nechama Leibowitz ranks among the most meaningful and long-lasting. I began my association with Professor Leibowitz in Tishrei 5733 (October 1972). I was among a group of approximately twenty students who studied with her twice weekly at Bet Midrash L'Torah, Jerusalem. Her lessons demanded thinking; students were required to answer questions in writing and approach her desk or be prepared for a visit to have their answers reviewed.

As the year progressed, our analytical skills developed and we gradually acquired the power of finding insights in texts with which we thought we had been familiar. Nechama Leibowitz enabled us to discover questions on the holy text and trained us to find solutions on our own. She also made the words of the commentators, particularly Rashi, come alive, enabling us to appreciate the basis for their disagreements.

In May 1973, we were no longer the same students that we had been at the start of the academic year. We began to anticipate missing the vitality of Nechama Leibowitz. At the conclusion of class one evening, we asked Nechama if she would come to the States to deliver some *shiurim* (classes). She turned to us and said, "I've been asked by Queens College to be a guest lecturer. Brooklyn College offered me a position and said it was the highest paying of the colleges. Yeshiva University asked me to lecture, and I told them what I will tell you. I have been in exile for twenty-five hundred years, now that I am back home, I am not leaving. If you wish to study Torah with me, you must come to Israel!"

It was my special privilege to communicate with Nechama Leibowitz over a period spanning twenty-four years. Our communication included the exchange of letters, phone conversations and personal visits. I was meticulous to write notes from each encounter. In this volume, I share some of the wisdom Nechama Leibowitz imparted to me in the hope that even those who were not able to travel to Israel to study with the master, will benefit from her Torah.

—Benjamin Saul Yasgur

Updates and revisions to this volume may be found at
www.ConversationswithNechama.com.

ACKNOWLEDGEMENTS

I EXTEND MY GRATITUDE TO THE FOLLOWING INDIVIDUALS: Tzvi Mauer, Publisher, for his valuable guidance; Ms. Sara Rosenbaum for her careful, patient and professional review of my manuscript; members of the Urim staff who worked diligently to bring this volume to print; Rabbi Yitshak Reiner for his assistance in reviewing Nechama Leibowitz's letter on living in the Diaspora.

THE FIRST FAMILY'S FIRST RESIDENCE

The Rule of The Distant Past (עָבָר רָחוֹק)

WHERE DID ADAM, EVE AND THEIR CHILDREN LIVE AS A family? The parents celebrated their marriage in the Garden of Eden and began life together there. Where were their children born?

A careful study of the events during and after the couple's life in the Garden of Eden will reveal an answer while establishing the Torah's view of the sanctity of marriage and its conjugal component. At the same time, such study will identify a rule of biblical grammar crucial to the understanding of several other biblical events.

The story of Adam's and Eve's experiences in the Garden of Eden appear to be contained in chapters 2 and 3 of Genesis. Chapter 3 ends with the couple's expulsion from the Garden of Eden for having disobeyed God's command.

Now the Lord God said, "Behold, man has become like one of us, having the ability of knowing good and evil, and now, lest he stretch forth his hand and take also from the Tree of Life and eat and live forever." The Lord God sent him out of the Garden of Eden to till the soil from where he had been taken. He drove the man out, and He stationed from the	וַיֹּאמֶר יְ־הוָֹה אֱ־לֹ־הִים הֵן הָאָדָם הָיָה כְּאַחַד מִמֶּנּוּ לָדַעַת טוֹב וָרָע וְעַתָּה פֶּן־יִשְׁלַח יָדוֹ וְלָקַח גַּם מֵעֵץ הַחַיִּים וְאָכַל וָחַי לְעֹלָם: וַיְשַׁלְּחֵהוּ יְ־הוָֹה אֱ־לֹ־הִים מִגַּן־עֵדֶן לַעֲבֹד אֶת־הָאֲדָמָה אֲשֶׁר לֻקַּח מִשָּׁם: וַיְגָרֶשׁ אֶת־הָאָדָם וַיַּשְׁכֵּן מִקֶּדֶם

From class at Beit Midrash L'Torah 5733/1973 and correspondence from Nechama Leibowitz dated 28 Tevet 5737/December 20, 1976.

east of the Garden of Eden the cherubim and the   לְגַן־עֵדֶן אֶת־הַכְּרֻבִים וְאֵת לַהַט

blade of the revolving sword to guard the way to the   הַחֶרֶב הַמִּתְהַפֶּכֶת לִשְׁמֹר אֶת־

Tree of Life. (Genesis 3:22–24)   דֶּרֶךְ עֵץ הַחַיִּים:

The account of life in the Garden of Eden as presented in Genesis 2 and 3
contains no reference to the conception or birth of children. The first clear
reference to marital intimacy between Adam and Eve occurs only after
their expulsion. As chapter 4 begins, we are told:

The Man knew Eve, his wife. She conceived and bore   וְהָאָדָם יָדַע אֶת־חַוָּה אִשְׁתּוֹ

Cain, saying, "This man shall be my acquisition for   וַתַּהַר וַתֵּלֶד אֶת־קַיִן וַתֹּאמֶר

the sake of God."[1] (Genesis 4:1)   קָנִיתִי אִישׁ אֶת־יְ־הֹוָה:

The order of the chapters and their events has led some schools of
Christianity to suggest that the sexual act, even within the context of marriage, is associated with a state of sin and only after human beings' fall from
the Garden of Eden. The Torah's view is quite different.

Rashi notes that the Hebrew grammatical construction of the two
opening words of Chapter 4, וְהָאָדָם יָדַע, "The Man knew," varies from the
normal biblical form. In regular usage, the verb precedes the noun. In the
examples which follow, the order of the subject and verb is preserved, even
though this literal translation sounds strange in English.

Said God, "Let there be light," and there was light.   וַיֹּאמֶר אֱ־לֹהִים יְהִי־אוֹר וַיְהִי

(Genesis 1:3)   אוֹר.

Knew Cain his wife; she conceived and bore Enoch,   וַיֵּדַע קַיִן אֶת־אִשְׁתּוֹ וַתַּהַר וַתֵּלֶד

and he was building a city; he called the city after   אֶת־חֲנוֹךְ וַיְהִי בֹּנֶה עִיר וַיִּקְרָא

the name of his son, Enoch. (Genesis 4:17)   שֵׁם הָעִיר כְּשֵׁם בְּנוֹ חֲנוֹךְ:

Did Noah according to all that God had com-   וַיַּעַשׂ נֹחַ כְּכֹל אֲשֶׁר צִוָּה אֹתוֹ

manded him; so did he. (Genesis 6:22)   אֱ־לֹהִים כֵּן עָשָׂה:

---

1 Translation follows the commentary of the Ramban.

When the Torah deviates from the norm by listing the subject first, it is telling us: stop, take note; something different is happening here. The reverse order of subject and verb often tells us that the action described occurred before the previously recorded event. Hence, regarding the sexual union between Adam and Eve, Rashi comments,

"This took place already before the above-mentioned story, before he sinned and was banished from the Garden of Eden; and similarly the conception and birth"[2] (Genesis 4:1).

The opening verse of chapter 4, which begins "The Man knew," is actually part of the events that occurred in the Garden of Eden as related in chapters 2 and 3. Adam and Eve wed in the Garden of Eden and bore children while they still lived there. The divine blessing, recorded immediately below, which was bestowed on God's human creation, found its initial fulfillment in the spiritual setting of the Garden of Eden.

God blessed them and God said to them, "Be fruitful and multiply and fill the earth and subdue it; and rule over the fish of the ocean and the birds of the sky and all living things that move on the earth." (Genesis 1:28)	וַיְבָרֶךְ אֹתָם אֱ־לֹהִים וַיֹּאמֶר לָהֶם אֱ־לֹהִים פְּרוּ וּרְבוּ וּמִלְאוּ אֶת־הָאָרֶץ וְכִבְשֻׁהָ וּרְדוּ בִּדְגַת הַיָּם וּבְעוֹף הַשָּׁמַיִם וּבְכָל־חַיָּה הָרֹמֶשֶׂת עַל־הָאָרֶץ׃

The challenge left to the reader is to understand why the Torah decided to place the verses announcing the conception and birth of Cain and Abel at the beginning of a new section rather than in chronological sequence.

★

Nechama Leibowitz termed Rashi's rule as *avar rahok* (עָבָר רָחוֹק), the distant

---

2 Rashi's opinion is consistent with the view of Rabbi Yohanan bar Hanina, as recorded in the Talmud, *Sanhedrin* 38b:

Rabbi Yohanan bar Hanina said: The day consisted of twelve hours. In the first hour, his [Adam's] dust was gathered; in the second, it was kneaded into a shapeless mass. In the third, his limbs were shaped; in the fourth, a soul was infused into him; in the fifth, he arose and stood on his feet; in the sixth, he gave [the animals] their names; in the seventh, Eve became his mate; in the eighth, they ascended to bed as two and descended as four; in the ninth, he was commanded not to eat of the tree, in the tenth, he sinned; in the eleventh, he was tried, and in the twelfth he was expelled [from Eden] and departed.

past, or *avar mi-kodem* (עָבָר מְקוֹדָם), the antecedent past. Other examples of this principle include:

The Lord remembered Sarah as He had said, and did the Lord to Sarah as He had spoken. (Genesis 21:1)	וַי־הֹוָ־ה פָּקַד אֶת־שָׂרָ־ה כַּאֲשֶׁר אָמָר וַיַּעַשׂ יְהֹוָ־ה לְשָׂרָה כַּאֲשֶׁר דִּבֵּר:

God's remembering Sarah and enabling her to conceive, and ultimately give birth, is recorded immediately after Abimelech's attempt to take Sarah by force as a wife. As a result of Abimelech's act, his household was stricken with a condition that, among other things, prevented the pregnant women in his palace from giving birth. After Sarah's release, Abraham prayed on behalf of the king's household and the punishment was lifted. The women bore their children. Rashi teaches that the use of *avar rahok* (וַי־הֹוָ־ה פָּקַד, "God remembered," instead of the normal construct, וַיִּפְקוֹד י־הֹוָ־ה, "remembered God") teaches that Sarah conceived before Abimelech's household recovered. The Talmud (*Bava Kama* 92a) uses this text as the source for our sages' statement, "He who prays for mercy for his friend when he needs the same thing is answered first."

Consider also Jacob's purchase of the birthright from Esau.

Said Esau to Jacob, "Pour into me, now, some of that very red stuff for I am exhausted"; called he, therefore, his name Edom. Said Jacob, "Sell, as this day, your birthright to me." Said Esau, "Look, I am going to die, so of what use to me is a birthright?" Said Jacob, "Swear to me as this day"; swore he to him and sold his birthright to Jacob. Jacob gave Esau bread and lentil stew, he ate and drank, got up and left; thus Esau spurned the birthright. (Genesis 25:30-34)	וַיֹּאמֶר עֵשָׂו אֶל־יַעֲקֹב הַלְעִיטֵנִי נָא מִן־הָאָדֹם הָאָדֹם הַזֶּה כִּי עָיֵף אָנֹכִי עַל־כֵּן קָרָא־שְׁמוֹ אֱדוֹם: וַיֹּאמֶר יַעֲקֹב מִכְרָה כַיּוֹם אֶת־בְּכֹרָתְךָ לִי: וַיֹּאמֶר עֵשָׂו הִנֵּה אָנֹכִי הוֹלֵךְ לָמוּת וְלָמָּה־זֶּה לִי בְּכֹרָה: וַיֹּאמֶר יַעֲקֹב הִשָּׁבְעָ־ה לִּי כַּיּוֹם וַיִּשָּׁבַע לוֹ וַיִּמְכֹּר אֶת־בְּכֹרָתוֹ לְיַעֲקֹב: וְיַעֲקֹב נָתַן לְעֵשָׂו לֶחֶם וּנְזִיד עֲדָשִׁים וַיֹּאכַל וַיֵּשְׁתְּ וַיָּקָם וַיֵּלַךְ וַיִּבֶז עֵשָׂו אֶת־הַבְּכֹרָה:

Was it fair for Jacob to extract the birthright from his famished brother? How hungry was Esau when he agreed to the sale? Notice that all the dialogues, except one, record the verb first. However, when the Torah declares that Jacob gave food to Esau, the subject noun is placed first. According to the rule of *avar rahok*, Jacob had already provided food to Esau before the birthright transaction! It is for this reason that the Torah declares, "Esau spurned the birthright." Even after his hunger was alleviated, he agreed to sell away his birthright.[3]

Nechama Leibowitz explained that not for every case in which the noun precedes the verb do we invoke the rule of the distant past. At times, the reversal from the usual form indicates an antithesis. Examples of this antithesis include:

| After a period of time, brought Cain[4] an offering to God of the fruit of the ground. And Abel, brought[5] he, too, of the firstlings of his flock and from their choicest, turned God to Abel and to his offering. (Genesis 4:3–5) | וַיְהִי מִקֵּץ יָמִים וַיָּבֵא קַיִן מִפְּרִי הָאֲדָמָה מִנְחָה לַיהוָה: וְהֶבֶל הֵבִיא גַם־הוּא מִבְּכֹרוֹת צֹאנוֹ וּמֵחֶלְבֵהֶן וַיִּשַׁע יְהוָה אֶל־הֶבֶל וְאֶל־מִנְחָתוֹ: וְאֶל־קַיִן וְאֶל־מִנְחָתוֹ לֹא שָׁעָה וַיִּחַר לְקַיִן מְאֹד וַיִּפְּלוּ פָּנָיו: |

In this instance, to emphasize that Abel's offering was on a higher level (he brought the choicest of the first-born animals) the Torah records his name prior to the verb. This reversal of syntax contrasts Abel and his brother. (The addition of the phrase גַם הוּא, "he too" clearly indicates that this action was second in order to that of Cain.[6])

A similar example of contrast may be found in Genesis 32:1–2:

| Arose Laban early in the morning, kissed he his sons and daughters and blessed them, then Laban went and returned to his place. Jacob went on his way and angels of God encountered him. | וַיַּשְׁכֵּם לָבָן בַּבֹּקֶר וַיְנַשֵּׁק לְבָנָיו וְלִבְנוֹתָיו וַיְבָרֶךְ אֶתְהֶם וַיֵּלֶךְ וַיָּשָׁב לָבָן לִמְקֹמוֹ: וְיַעֲקֹב הָלַךְ לְדַרְכּוֹ וַיִּפְגְּעוּ־בוֹ מַלְאֲכֵי אֱלֹהִים: |

Jacob's departure occurred after Laban kissed his sons and daughters and after Laban took leave. The placement of the noun first is for antithetical

---

3 This thought is an observation of the author based on Rashi's principle of *avar rahok*.

4 Syntax left awkward to emphasize the antecedent position of the verb, the usual biblical form.

5 Note that the noun precedes the action.

6 Thought based on author's observation.

emphasis and helps to introduce a new stage in the life of Jacob.[7,8] Awareness of the nuances of biblical grammar brings added dimension to one's understanding of the events in the Bible. At times, the implication can be monumental.

---

7 Thought based on author's observation.

8 I discussed with Nechama Leibowitz (on 16 Adar I 5757/February 23, 1997) two examples of verb and subject reversal that are not cases of the Distant Past. In Genesis 46:28, we read:

וְאֶת־יְהוּדָה שָׁלַח לְפָנָיו אֶל־יוֹסֵף לְהוֹרֹת לְפָנָיו גֹּשְׁנָה וַיָּבֹאוּ אַרְצָה גֹּשֶׁן:

Judah, he sent before him unto Joseph, to show the way before him to Goshen; they came into the land of Goshen.

To qualify as a case of Distant Past, Nechama explained, the text must contain a subject followed by a direct object (of that subject's action). Here, it is Jacob who is sending Judah, but, as his name does not appear in the verse, we do not have the technical requirements of the Distant Past. I do note, though, as verse 6 in this chapter already tells us that

וַיָּבֹאוּ מִצְרַיְמָה יַעֲקֹב וְכָל־זַרְעוֹ אִתּוֹ:

they came to Egypt, Jacob and all his offspring with him

and the arrival is restated in verse 27, it is obvious that this action, too, happened earlier in time than its textual placement.

In Genesis 19:1 we read:

וַיָּבֹאוּ שְׁנֵי הַמַּלְאָכִים סְדֹמָה בָּעֶרֶב וְלוֹט יֹשֵׁב בְּשַׁעַר־סְדֹם וַיַּרְא־לוֹט וַיָּקָם לִקְרָאתָם וַיִּשְׁתַּחוּ אַפַּיִם אָרְצָה:

The two angels came to Sodom in the evening and Lot was sitting at the gate of Sodom; Lot saw them, rose up to greet them and he bowed, face to the earth.

As the verb in this verse is in the present tense, it cannot technically be a case of the Distant Past. Yet Nechama explained the phrase of וְלוֹט יֹשֵׁב, Lot was sitting, as conveying the meaning "he customarily sat there, he was already a judge by them."

I would add an additional example. In Exodus 24:1 we read:

וְאֶל־מֹשֶׁה אָמַר עֲלֵה אֶל־יְ-הוָה אַתָּה וְאַהֲרֹן נָדָב וַאֲבִיהוּא וְשִׁבְעִים מִזִּקְנֵי יִשְׂרָאֵל וְהִשְׁתַּחֲוִיתֶם מֵרָחֹק:

Unto Moses, He said, "Come up unto the Lord, you, and Aaron, Nadab, and Abihu, and seventy of the elders of Israel; and you shall bow from a distance.

Similar to our first example above, the actual subject (God) is not recorded in the verse; we are lacking the technical requirements for the Distant Past. Yet, Rashi opines that this verse and section are, indeed out of chronological order and occurred earlier!

We have, therefore, three examples of phrases containing an aberration in the usual placement of the verb; while not technically qualifying for examples of the Distant Past, they nevertheless do connote events which have a basis in time earlier than the chronological order of the text.

The following is a translation of an excerpt from a letter written by Nechama Leibowitz. The original Hebrew is transcribed below; a copy of the handwritten letter is also included in this chapter.

B"H 28 Tevet (5747)

Dear Benjamin, I was very happy with your letter. The questions are all truly questions about which one must reflect.

I will begin with Rashi's rule on *avar rahok*, the one that Rashi cites on Genesis 4:1 on the words "Adam knew [his wife]." On this [principle] is also built his explanation to Genesis 21:1 on the words "God remembered [Sarah]."

Similarly with 31:34, "Rachel took." Refer to my book *The Study of Biblical Commentators and Ways to Teach Them,*[1] page 1. This is an accepted rule, also by modern scholars.

But Rashi does *not* say that *every* place the Torah says "Peloni[2] did"[3] – its meaning is one of *avar rahok*, that the action was already done beforehand. On the contrary! If Scripture wants to say that the action was performed prior to the last recorded event, it uses the format of "Peloni did." Did you understand? (One who says all kohanim are from the tribe of Levi did *not*

---

1 This Hebrew volume has been republished with the title הוראת פרשני התורה *Teaching the Biblical Commentators.*

2 Peloni is the Hebrew equivalent of "John Doe."

3 I.e., placing the subject first, followed by the verb, in contrast to the usual biblical format of placing the verb first.

declare by this that *everyone* who is from the tribe of Levi is a kohen. And one who says that "women" belong to the category of "humans" did not say that every "human" is a woman.)

This format of "Peloni did" in place of "did Peloni"[4] appears, as well, when there is an antithesis in the verse. For example, "Brought Cain[5] from the fruits of the ground an offering to God. And Abel brought as well, from the firstborn of his sheep and from their fats" (Genesis 4:2–3). It does not mean that Abel brought [an offering] before Cain did.

And similarly in Genesis 32:1–2, "Went and returned Laban . . . And Jacob went . . . ." – These two places are not [examples of] antecedent past. Rather, the format expresses the *antithesis*.

With blessing,
—Nechama Leibowitz

---

4 i.e., the usual biblical format of the verb preceding the subject.

5 The order of the verb and subject as it appears in the biblical text has been preserved in this translation even though it may appear awkward in English.

ב"ה כ"ח בטבת

בנימין היקר, שמחתי מאוד במכתבך. שאלות באמת כלן שאלות שיש להרהר בהן.

אתחיל בכללו של רש"י על עבר רחוק. זה שרש"י מביא בבר' ד' א' ד"ה והאדם ידע ועל זה בנוי גם פרושו לכא' א' ד"ה וה' פקד.

וכן בר' ל"א לד ד"ה ורחל לקחה. ועיין בספרי למוד פרשני התורה ודרכים להוראתם עמוד 1. וזה כלל המקובל גם אצל חוקרים מודרניים.

אבל רש"י <u>לא</u> אומר <u>שבכל</u> מקום שנאמר "ופלוני עשה"- פרושו עבר רחוק, כבר עשה לפני כן. אלא להפך! אם רוצה הכתוב לומר שהדבר נעשה לפני המסופר לאחרונה הוא משתמש בצורה של"ופלוני עשה"- האם הבנת? (האומר שכל הכהנים הם משבט לוי <u>לא</u> אמר בזה <u>שכל</u> מי שהוא משבט לוי הוא כהן. והאומר ש"נשים" שייכות לסוג "אדם", לא אמר שכל "אדם"-אשה.)

הצורה הזו "ופלוני עשה" במקום "ויעש פלוני" מופיעה גם כשיש אנטי-תזה בפסוק.

כגון "ויבא קין מפרי . . . והבל הביא" אין פרושו שהבל הביא לפני קין.

וכן לב א-ב וילד (לבן) וישב ויעקב הלך". בשני המקומות האלה אין זה עבר מקודם אלא הצורה מבטאת את <u>הנגוד</u>.

בברכה,

נחמה ליבוביץ

Hebrew transcription of letter from Nechama Leibowitz

Photocopy of original, handwritten letter

DID MOSES THWART GOD'S PLAN?

A Study of the Application of *Avar Rahok*

M OSES STOOD IN AWE AT THE SITE OF THE BURNING BUSH. Even as he hears God's attempt to appoint him leader of the enslaved Israelites, Moses offers many reasons as to why he is not the ideal candidate. God insists and Moses relents. At some point after Moses's return to his father-in-law's home, the Torah tells us:

The Lord said to Moses in Midian, "Go, return to Egypt, for all the people who seek your life have died." (Exodus 4:19)	וַיֹּאמֶר יְהֹוָה אֶל־מֹשֶׁה בְּמִדְיָן לֵךְ שֻׁב מִצְרָיִם כִּי־מֵתוּ כָּל־הָאֲנָשִׁים הַמְבַקְשִׁים אֶת־נַפְשֶׁךָ׃

Who are these people who sought Moses's life? It would seem that the obvious answer is Pharaoh, whose death is recorded immediately before the account of the burning bush.

Now it came to pass in those many days that the king of Egypt died, and the children of Israel sighed from the labor, and they cried out, and their cry ascended to God from the labor. Moses was pasturing the flocks of Jethro, his father-in-law, the Chief of Midian; he led the flocks far into the wilderness, and he came to the mountain of God, to Horeb. An	וַיְהִי בַיָּמִים הָרַבִּים הָהֵם וַיָּמָת מֶלֶךְ מִצְרַיִם וַיֵּאָנְחוּ בְנֵי־יִשְׂרָאֵל מִן־הָעֲבֹדָה וַיִּזְעָקוּ וַתַּעַל שַׁוְעָתָם אֶל־הָאֱלֹהִים מִן־הָעֲבֹדָה: וּמֹשֶׁה הָיָה רֹעֶה אֶת־צֹאן יִתְרוֹ חֹתְנוֹ כֹּהֵן מִדְיָן וַיִּנְהַג אֶת־הַצֹּאן אַחַר הַמִּדְבָּר וַיָּבֹא אֶל־הַר הָאֱלֹהִים

From correspondence dated 18 Tevet 5737/December 20, 1976, and conversation with Nechama Leibowitz 12 Adar, 5756/March 3, 1996.

angel of the Lord appeared to him in a flame of fire from within the thorn bush, and behold, the thorn bush was burning with fire, but the thorn bush was not being consumed. (Exodus 2:23–3:2)

חֹרֵבָה: וַיֵּרָא מַלְאַךְ יְהוָֹה אֵלָיו בְּלַבַּת־אֵשׁ מִתּוֹךְ הַסְּנֶה וַיַּרְא וְהִנֵּה הַסְּנֶה בֹּעֵר בָּאֵשׁ וְהַסְּנֶה אֵינֶנּוּ אֻכָּל:

Indeed, the Ibn Ezra states that Pharaoh was the one seeking Moses's life. The plural reference in 4:19, "all the people," includes his advisers, who had also died in the meantime. However, Rashi, in his commentary on this verse, disagrees:

> "Who were they? Dathan and Abiram. They were alive, but they lost their property, and a pauper is considered dead."
>
> (Talmud *Nedarim* 64b)

Why would Rashi deviate from the apparent plain meaning to record a metaphoric explanation of death?

In December 1976 (Tevet 5737), I wrote to Nechama Leibowitz to propose that the application of the *avar rahok* principle – or the lack of it – might explain the basis of this dispute between Rashi and the Ibn Ezra.

The opening verse of Exodus 3 states:

Moses was pasturing the flocks of Jethro, his father-in-law, the Chief of Midian. He led the flocks far into the wilderness, and he came to the mountain of God, to Horeb. (Exodus 3:1)

וּמֹשֶׁה הָיָה רֹעֶה אֶת־צֹאן יִתְרוֹ חֹתְנוֹ כֹּהֵן מִדְיָן וַיִּנְהַג אֶת־הַצֹּאן אַחַר הַמִּדְבָּר וַיָּבֹא אֶל־הַר הָאֱלֹהִים חֹרֵבָה:

Note that contrary to normal biblical usage, the subject (Moses) precedes the verb in the above verse. If we understand the phrase וּמֹשֶׁה הָיָה רֹעֶה, "Moses was pasturing," as an instance of *avar rahok*, Moses's tending to the flock, the burning bush and (likely) God's command to return to Egypt all precede Pharaoh's death. Therefore, Rashi was forced to find another explanation for the plain meaning of the text.

Nechama Leibowitz rejected my suggestion. She said the factor that motivated Rashi to identify those who had "died" as Dathan and Abiram – who were actually alive – is the terminology that the Torah uses: "those who seek" (הַמְבַקְשִׁים). The present tense indicates the action is currently under way. Dathan and Abiram are perpetual antagonists. They continue their campaign against Moses, but no one pays attention to them because they have lost their wealth and their influence along with it.

Twice more I argued for the application of the *avar rahok* principle to this verse. Each time, Nechama rejected my idea. Two decades later, I renewed my proposal, this time suggesting that the *avar rahok* explanation served a purpose.

I shared with Nechama Leibowitz a thought from Rabbi Joseph B. Soloveitchik zt"l. In a lecture entitled "The Philosophy of Prayer," the Rav suggested that God is often prepared to provide humans with what that they need, but they must ask Him first. The human being must recognize that something is lacking and articulate this need. Only after one has put one's need into words does one truly understand it, and only then is God more committed to a positive response.

During the time of the Egyptian slavery, the Israelites did not sense the immorality of their enslavement. They accepted their status in silence. Moses was the first to highlight the injustice by striking the Egyptian taskmaster. The Israelites' first expression of dissatisfaction with their lot follows the death of Pharaoh. It is then that the nation groaned and cried to God.

"God heard their cry," the Torah tells us. "God remembered His covenant with Abraham, with Isaac, and with Jacob. God saw the children of Israel, and God knew" (Exodus 2:24–25).

What happened then? The Torah records that while Moses was pasturing Jethro's flock, he happened upon the burning bush. At first, Moses did not agree to God's request that he lead the Jewish people out of slavery. Offering a string of reasons why he was not the proper choice, Moses, according to the Midrash, extended the dialogue between himself and God for seven days.

Imagine the scene. After decades of enslavement, the Israelites ask God for relief. God is prepared to initiate the process of redemption through His designated emissary, Moses. But Moses is unwilling. Did Moses thwart God's plan? According to Ibn Ezra's reading of the verse, one would have to say yes: Moses was responsible for delaying God's plan for His people's salvation.

However, according to Rashi, with the application of the rule of *avar rahok*, the episode at the burning bush occurred before Pharaoh's death. By the time Pharaoh died, Moses had already accepted God's appointment and may even have been on the road to Egypt. There was no delay. As soon as the Jewish nation cried out with the recognition that something was wrong in their lives and that only God could help, God put His plan of response into immediate action.

As the episode of the burning bush occurred before Pharaoh's death, God could not have been referring to him when he said: "Go, return to Egypt, for all the people who seek your life have died." Hence, Rashi suggests that Moses's antagonists were Dathan and Abiram.

After my twenty-year campaign, Nechama Leibowitz accepted my suggestion.[1]

---

1 I later discovered that the Malbim, in his commentary to Exodus 3:1, also identifies the phrase וּמֹשֶׁה הָיָה רֹעֶה ("Moses was pasturing") as an example of *avar rahok*.

RECOGNIZING AN ENCOUNTER

WITH GOD

ONE OF THE MOST FAMOUS EPISODES IN THE TORAH PRESENTS Abraham sitting at the entrance to his tent on an extremely hot day. According to the Talmud (*Bava Metzia* 86b), Abraham was recuperating from his *brit milah* (circumcision). In fact, our sages say that it was the third and most painful day of recuperation. God appears to Abraham in this setting. Why? Why, we may also ask, does the Torah choose to share this encounter with us?

Strangely absent from the Torah's record of this event is a statement from the Almighty. While the Torah states, "God appeared to him [Abraham]," nowhere are we told what, if anything, God said to him. Nechama Leibowitz endorsed the opinion that God did not say anything. The whole purpose of God's appearance, said Nechama, was for God to be present with Abraham, to be at his side during the healing process.

The foundation for the concept of a silent appearance, explained Nechama, is found in the Ramban's commentary to Genesis 18:1. The Torah states:

God appeared to him on the Plains of Mamre and he was sitting at the entrance of the tent in the heat of the day.

וַיֵּרָא אֵלָיו יְ־הוָֹה בְּאֵלֹנֵי מַמְרֵא וְהוּא יֹשֵׁב פֶּתַח־הָאֹהֶל כְּחֹם הַיּוֹם:

The Ramban observes, "Divine revelation here . . . is not for the purpose

From conversation with Nechama Leibowitz on 3 Tevet 5753/December 27, 1992.

of commanding them a mitzvah nor is it intended at all to convey a spoken message. Rather, it is a reward for the mitzvah already completed [the *brit milah*] and to inform them that God was pleased with their actions."

Why does the Torah record the episode? It does so in order to teach us a lesson for all time. God's intent was to keep Abraham company. Yet, upon seeing wayfarers, Abraham takes leave of God to perform the act of *hachnasat orhim* (hospitality).

We learn from here, Nechama stated, that "it is more important to offer help. The simple act of giving water is greater than Divine revelation!"

ELIEZER'S MISSION

Eliezer accepted a two-part mission from Abraham. He agreed to identify an appropriate woman from his master's homeland to marry Isaac. He also agreed to try to convince her to relocate to Canaan.

After Eliezer accepts the responsibility and swears to the conditions imposed by Abraham, the Torah tells us:

The servant took ten camels from his master's camels and went	וַיִּקַּח הָעֶבֶד עֲשָׂרָה גְמַלִּים מִגְּמַלֵּי אֲדֹנָיו וַיֵּלֶךְ
and all of his master's bounty were in his hand;	וְכָל־טוּב אֲדֹנָיו בְּיָדוֹ
he stood up and went	וַיָּקָם וַיֵּלֶךְ
to Aram Naharayim, to the city of Nahor.	אֶל־אֲרַם נַהֲרַיִם אֶל־עִיר נָחוֹר:

These four phrases comprise one verse in the Torah (Genesis 24:10). They are laid out in sections, as Nechama frequently did, to help the reader identify the question: How many times did Eliezer actually set out on his mission? Even though the Torah says twice that he "went," it is unlikely that he actually set out twice.

The structure of the verse sets apart and emphasizes the selection of the ten camels. I suggested to Nechama Leibowitz that the main challenge facing Eliezer was to find the woman worthy of marrying Isaac and becoming

---

From conversation with Nechama Leibowitz on 8 Tevet 5755/December 11, 1994.

a matriarch in the nation of Abraham's descendants. Eliezer did not set out until he had a plan in mind. While still in his master's home, Eliezer developed a strategy to test the quality of *hesed* (kindness) of a potential spouse. The camels were the centerpiece of the plan. Once Eliezer had a vision of the stratagem, he was mentally ready to set out on his mission. The Torah alerts us to this development by recording the first "he went." But it was not meant to convey a description of a physical action. Eliezer had other preparations to make before he set out. The Torah tells us that once he completed these tasks, he stood up and went to Aram Naharayim, to the city of Nahor. Nechama accepted my suggestion, saying, "It's very feasible. I like it."

This approach to understanding the verse reflects favorably on Eliezer, especially in light of the view of the Midrash that Eliezer hoped that his own daughter would marry Isaac. Even though he was personally disappointed, he performed Abraham's bidding with diligence. He did not set out in a haphazard manner, but planned to the best of his ability to be successful in his commitment to Abraham.

E LIEZER WAS CONVINCED THAT HE HAD IDENTIFIED A SUIT-
able wife for Isaac. Therefore, he bedecked Rebecca with valuable
jewelry, questioned her about her lineage and asked about possible
lodging for himself and his animals. When Rebecca runs home to report
these events, the text introduces us to her brother, Laban. What can we learn
about Laban's personality and values from the Torah's initial description?

Genesis 24:28–30 tells us:

28. The girl ran and told her mother's household these things.	(כח) וַתָּרָץ הַנַּעֲרָ֯ וַתַּגֵּד לְבֵית אִמָּהּ כַּדְּבָרִים הָאֵלֶּה:
29. Rebecca had a brother whose name was Laban. Laban ran out to the man, to the well.	(כט) וּלְרִבְקָה אָח וּשְׁמוֹ לָ֯בָן וַיָּרָץ לָבָן אֶל־הָאִישׁ הַחוּצָה אֶל־הָעָיִן:
30. And it came to pass that when he saw the earring and bracelets upon his sister's hands, and when he heard the words of Rebecca his sister, saying, "Thus spoke the man to me," that he approached to the man; and behold, he stood by the camels at the well.	(ל) וַיְהִי כִּרְאֹת אֶת־הַנֶּ֯זֶם וְאֶת־הַצְּמִדִים עַל־יְדֵי אֲחֹתוֹ וּכְשָׁמְעוֹ אֶת־דִּבְרֵ֯י רִבְקָה אֲחֹתוֹ֯ לֵאמֹר כֹּה־דִבֶּר֯ אֵלַי הָאִישׁ וַיָּבֹ֯א אֶל־הָאִישׁ וְהִנֵּה עֹמֵד עַל־הַגְּמַלִּ֯ים עַל־הָעָיִן:

As soon as we are informed of Laban's existence, he is off and running to
greet Eliezer. Is he as eager to welcome guests as his great-uncle Abraham?

Hardly. As Rashi teaches, the purpose of the strange order of the verses is

---

From conversation with Nechama Leibowitz on 18 Shevat 5757/January 26, 1997.

meant to convey an unequivocal understanding of what motivated Laban. It was not the opportunity to welcome guests, nor was it excitement over his sister's good fortune. It was, as the final verse above implies, the lure of riches.

Why is there an apparent clash in the verbs that describe Laban's movement? First we are told that he "ran." Then we are told that "he approached." Nechama Leibowitz accepted my suggestion that Laban attempted to conceal his enthusiasm for fear that Eliezer might suspect Laban's interest in the wealth that he carried. So while Laban runs at the beginning, it is only הַחוּצָה "to the outside." He runs out of his house but, as Laban nears Eliezer, his pattern shifts to וַיָּבֹא, "he approached," in a calm, nonchalant manner.[1] (For another example of a change of pace between running and walking, see Genesis 39:12 and the Seforno's commentary there.[2])

When Laban approaches Eliezer, why is it necessary for the Torah to add "behold, he [Eliezer] stood by the camels"? It should have been sufficient to say: he approached the man at the well. Nechama explained that the Torah is emphasizing the real focus of Laban – the camels and the wealth that they carry. For Laban, the guest's arrival presents an opportunity for financial gain.

Returning to the verses describing Laban's reaction, we must confront an apparent question of sequence. Once Laban ran out to Eliezer, how can

---

1 Compare Laban's actions to those of Abraham when he greeted his three guests:
וַיִּשָּׂא עֵינָיו וַיַּרְא וְהִנֵּה שְׁלֹשָׁה אֲנָשִׁים נִצָּבִים עָלָיו וַיַּרְא וַיָּרָץ לִקְרָאתָם מִפֶּתַח הָאֹהֶל וַיִּשְׁתַּחוּ אָרְצָה:
"He lifted up his eyes and looked, and, lo, three men stood by him; he saw, ran to meet them from the tent door, and bowed himself to the ground." (Genesis 18:2)
Notice that Abraham runs the full distance to his guests and does not conceal his eagerness to welcome them.

2   וַתִּתְפְּשֵׂהוּ בְּבִגְדוֹ לֵאמֹר שִׁכְבָה עִמִּי וַיַּעֲזֹב בִּגְדוֹ בְּיָדָהּ וַיָּנָס וַיֵּצֵא הַחוּצָה.
"She grabbed him by his garment, saying, 'Lie with me'; he left his garment in her hand and fled and went outside."
The Seforno explains that Joseph initially runs, to get out of the room in which he is accosted by Potiphar's wife. He is eager to avoid her sexual advances. Once Joseph escapes her clutch, he adopts a normal walking pace in order to avoid being asked by others why he is fleeing. The Seforno implies that Joseph had no intention, as a slave, to report the incident. Potiphar's wife, however, only sees Joseph fleeing, observes the Seforno. (Author's comment: As Potiphar's wife assumes Joseph will be questioned, she launches an offensive to malign Joseph and portray herself as an innocent victim.)

the text inform us that "he saw the earring and bracelets upon his sister's hands," and so on? If Laban already ran outside, he could no longer be observing and listening to Rebecca!

The Torah is using the flashback technique. Indeed, first Laban saw his sister wearing the jewelry and heard her remarks, and only then ran to the well to greet Eliezer. Why not state the events as they occurred? The early description of Laban's haste to reach the source of the jewels conveys his focus on the gifts. Once the Torah succeeds in establishing this tone, the text returns to fill in the details. The result is a finely choreographed depiction of Laban's greed.[3]

---

3 I did not have the opportunity to share this observation with Nechama Leibowitz.

JACOB'S MASQUERADE

ID JACOB DO WRONG?
Under pressure from his mother, Jacob disguised himself as Esau
in an effort to receive his father's blessing. Isaac, his eyesight failing
and sensing that his years might be nearing their end, summoned his firstborn, Esau, and commanded him to hunt deer and prepare venison for him.
While Esau was out fulfilling his mission, Jacob went to Isaac with a meal
freshly prepared by his mother, Rebecca. When Isaac asked him to identify
himself; Jacob answered:

I am Esau, your firstborn. I have done as you told   אָנֹכִי עֵשָׂו בְּכֹרֶךָ עָשִׂיתִי כַּאֲשֶׁר
me. (Genesis 27:19)   דִּבַּרְתָּ אֵלָי

Jacob succeeded in securing the blessing intended for his brother. When
Esau returned and discovered the masquerade, he cried out with an exceedingly bitter cry and resolved to kill his brother after Isaac's death.

Our sages paint Esau as a scoundrel, guilty of terrible crimes. Rebecca
felt that Esau was unworthy of Isaac's blessing. May we conclude that Jacob
and Rebecca were justified in arranging the masquerade?

I shared with Nechama Leibowitz the isolation I felt in analyzing the
message of the episode. When I remarked how educators and others defend
Jacob's masquerade, she grew indignant. "He will definitely pay for this,"
she said. "The punishment is awesome. It was with him his entire life." As

---

From conversation with Nechama Leibowitz on 7 Tevet 5754/December 21, 1993.

a result of his action, Jacob was deceived in his attempt to marry Rachel. He married two women and had children by both. Jacob's preference for Rachel's offspring over Leah's caused hatred among his sons. This enmity led the brothers to sell Joseph into slavery and deceive Jacob into thinking that Joseph was dead. Refusing all comfort, Jacob bore his grief for more than two decades. (It is possible that even today, we still bear the scars of hatred between Jews.[1])

What about the Divine message to Rebecca that Jacob was to be the heir to Isaac's and Abraham's covenant with God? "The end does not justify the means. There could have been other options available to achieve the goal in a proper fashion," Nechama explained. "The mechanism that Jacob chose does not convert deception into a kosher act. He followed a path of deception; there is no pardon. God punished him and he suffered his whole life."

In *Studies in the Book of Genesis* (Hebrew edition, page 185), Nechama Leibowitz observed that Scripture rarely places a direct value statement on actions. Rather, the context and ensuing events reflect the appropriateness of an episode. Therefore, the Bible includes some narratives as a basis for understanding future developments or as a lesson of what not to do. Jacob's deception would be among them.

Nechama Leibowitz understood our sages' view as critical of Jacob's masquerade. They interpret Laban's trick on Jacob's wedding day as a Divine act of retribution that was meted out measure for measure: as Jacob had deceived his father, so Laban deceived him. Our sages speak through the voice of Leah in *Midrash Tanhuma Yashan* (Va-yetze 11):

All that night she [Leah] acted the part of Rachel. As soon as he arose in the morning, "and behold it was Leah," he [Jacob] said to her, "Daughter of the deceiver! Why have you deceived me?" She said to him, "And you, why did you deceive your father?! When he said to you, 'Are you my son Esau?' you said to him, 'I am Esau, your first-born.' Yet you say, 'Why have you deceived me?!' Did your father not say of you, 'Your brother came in deceit'"?

---

1 Author's observation.

Our Sages' view finds expression in our very Torah text! When the Torah
shares with us that Laban had two daughters, we are told

Now Laban had two daughters: the name of the bigger one was Leah, and the name of the smaller one was Rachel. (Genesis 29:16)	וּלְלָבָן שְׁתֵּי בָנוֹת שֵׁם הַגְּדֹלָה לֵאָה וְשֵׁם הַקְּטַנָּה רָחֵל:

Notice that Leah is referred to as the bigger sister and Rachel as the smaller
sibling. Yet, on the morning following the wedding, as Jacob registers his
surprise with his new father-in-law, Laban's response is worded differently:

Laban said, "It is not so done in our place, to give the younger before the firstborn." (Genesis 29:26)	וַיֹּאמֶר לָבָן לֹא-יֵעָשֶׂה כֵן בִּמְקוֹמֵנוּ לָתֵת הַצְּעִירָה לִפְנֵי הַבְּכִירָה:

Laban is not using the original term of הַגְּדֹלָה, the bigger one; rather, he
is using a code word, הַבְּכִירָה, the first born. Laban becomes the voice to
identify Jacob's masquerade as a sin against his father.

Unfortunately for Jacob and his descendants, there would be multiple
measures of repayment against his single act of deception. Rabbi Hanina,
in *Midrash Rabbah* (Genesis 67:4), teaches:

> Whoever maintains that The Holy One, blessed be He, is a foregoer
> [of His just claims], may he forego his life! He is merely long-suffer-
> ing, but [ultimately] collects His due. Jacob made Esau break out into
> a cry but once . . . and where was he punished for it? In Shushan, the
> capital, as it says, "He cried out with a loud and bitter cry." (Esther 4:1)

To emphasize the consequences of Jacob's masquerade, I refer to a public lecture that Rabbi Joseph Soloveitchik delivered on 10 Tevet 5741/
December 16, 1980. The Rav noted that God's covenant with Abraham
stipulated, "Know with certainty that your offspring will be aliens in a
land not their own. They will serve them, and they will oppress them for
four hundred years" (Genesis 15:13). We were destined to serve a foreign
people in a strange land; but, the name of the land was not recorded. Note

also that our ancestors did not complete the four hundred years of servitude. Our stay in Egypt lasted for two hundred and ten years from the time Jacob took his family to Egypt. Our time of servitude was even less than that because as long as Jacob and his sons were alive, the Jews living in Egypt enjoyed freedom and prosperity. (In order to fulfill the prophecy of four hundred years, our sages began the count with the birth of Isaac, who never left Israel.)

Jacob spent approximately twenty years in Haran, also a "land not [his] own." He served Laban under harsh and often unfair conditions. God, who regularly accepts partial payment as complete restitution of a debt, was prepared to accept Jacob's existence outside the Promised Land as the fulfillment of the condition set with Abraham.[2] Jacob returned to Israel with the intention of never leaving. He had completed the destined conditions of exile and servitude. This is why the Torah states:

Jacob settled in the land of his father's sojourning, in the land of Canaan. (Genesis 37:1)	וַיֵּשֶׁב יַעֲקֹב בְּאֶרֶץ מְגוּרֵי אָבִיו בְּאֶרֶץ כְּנָעַן:

Why did the Torah add the apparently superfluous description of "the land of his father's sojourning"? Rav Soloveitchik explained that this was in order to emphasize that Jacob was coming to the land that Jews would never again leave in exile, just as his father, Isaac, had never left. Jacob was prepared to be the vehicle for the implementation of the Divine promises offered to Abraham.

Esau too, understood this, as it is written:

Esau took his wives, his sons, his daughters, and all the members of his household, his livestock and all his animals, and all the wealth he had acquired in the land of Canaan, and went to a land because of his brother Jacob. (Genesis 36:6)	וַיִּקַּח עֵשָׂו אֶת־נָשָׁיו וְאֶת־בָּנָיו וְאֶת־בְּנֹתָיו וְאֶת־כָּל־נַפְשׁוֹת בֵּיתוֹ וְאֶת־מִקְנֵהוּ וְאֶת־כָּל־בְּהֶמְתּוֹ וְאֵת כָּל־קִנְיָנוֹ אֲשֶׁר רָכַשׁ בְּאֶרֶץ כְּנָעַן וַיֵּלֶךְ אֶל־אֶרֶץ מִפְּנֵי יַעֲקֹב אָחִיו:

---

2 See also *On Repentance*, 270–294, where Rav Soloveitchik presents the basis for partial repayment canceling entire debts.

Esau equated Jacob's return to the conquest of Canaan. Esau yielded and departed.

The forty-three verses recorded immediately prior to the statement of Jacob's settling in Canaan provide a detailed genealogy of Esau's family. They establish Esau's claim to Mount Seir and his departure from Canaan. According to the original Divine plan, said Rav Soloveitchik, the Jews were never supposed to go down to Egypt!

What changed the course of Jewish history? The sale of Joseph. What caused the sale of Joseph? Jacob's masquerade!

UPON LEARNING OF ISAAC'S PLAN TO BLESS ESAU, REBECCA devises a scheme to ensure that Jacob receives the blessing. From the time that she summons Jacob through Jacob's arrival before his father, Jacob initiates four actions. A quick review of the verses below shows that Jacob's name is mentioned only in one of the four instances of action.

Rebecca was listening as Isaac spoke to Esau, his son; Esau went to the field to hunt game to bring. Rebecca spoke to Jacob, her son, saying: "Behold, I heard your father speaking to Esau, your brother, saying, 'Bring me game and prepare for me delicacies that I will eat, and I will bless you in the presence of God before my death.' And now, my son, hearken to my voice regarding what I command you. Go, please, to the flock and fetch for me from there two good kids from among the goats, and I will prepare them as delicacies for your father, such as he loves. Then you will bring [them] to your father that he may eat; in order that he shall bless you before his death." **Jacob replied** to Rebecca, his mother, "Behold, Esau my brother is a hairy man, and I am a smooth man. Maybe my father will feel

וְרִבְקָה שֹׁמַעַת בְּדַבֵּר יִצְחָק אֶל־
עֵשָׂו בְּנוֹ וַיֵּלֶךְ עֵשָׂו הַשָּׂדֶה לָצוּד
צַיִד לְהָבִיא: וְרִבְקָה אָמְרָה אֶל־
יַעֲקֹב בְּנָהּ לֵאמֹר הִנֵּה שָׁמַעְתִּי
אֶת־אָבִיךָ מְדַבֵּר אֶל־עֵשָׂו אָחִיךָ
לֵאמֹר: הָבִיאָה לִּי צַיִד וַעֲשֵׂה־לִי
מַטְעַמִּים וְאֹכֵלָה וַאֲבָרֶכְכָה לִפְנֵי
יְהֹוָה לִפְנֵי מוֹתִי: וְעַתָּה בְנִי שְׁמַע
בְּקֹלִי לַאֲשֶׁר אֲנִי מְצַוָּה אֹתָךְ:
לֶךְ־נָא אֶל־הַצֹּאן וְקַח־לִי מִשָּׁם
שְׁנֵי גְּדָיֵי עִזִּים טֹבִים וְאֶעֱשֶׂה
אֹתָם מַטְעַמִּים לְאָבִיךָ כַּאֲשֶׁר
אָהֵב: וְהֵבֵאתָ לְאָבִיךָ וְאָכָל בַּעֲבֻר
אֲשֶׁר יְבָרֶכְךָ לִפְנֵי מוֹתוֹ: וַיֹּאמֶר
יַעֲקֹב אֶל־רִבְקָה אִמּוֹ הֵן עֵשָׂו
אָחִי אִישׁ שָׂעִר וְאָנֹכִי אִישׁ חָלָק:

From correspondence with Nechama Leibowitz dated Heshvan 5752/November 1991.

me and I will be in his eyes a misleader; and I will bring upon myself a curse and not a blessing." His mother said to him, "Upon me be your curse, my son. Only obey my voice and go fetch for me." **He went, he took and he brought** [them] to his mother; his mother prepared delicacies as his father loved. Rebecca took the coveted garments of Esau, her older son, which were with her in the house, and dressed Jacob, her younger son. And the skins of the kids of the goats she placed on his hands and on the smoothness of his neck. She gave the delicacies and the bread which she made into the hand of Jacob, her son. **He came** to his father and **said**, "My father." He said, "Here I am. Who are you, my son?" (Genesis 27:5–18)

אוּלַי יְמֻשֵּׁנִי אָבִי וְהָיִיתִי בְעֵינָיו כִּמְתַעְתֵּעַ וְהֵבֵאתִי עָלַי קְלָלָה וְלֹא בְרָכָה: וַתֹּאמֶר לוֹ אִמּוֹ עָלַי קִלְלָתְךָ בְּנִי אַךְ שְׁמַע בְּקֹלִי וְלֵךְ קַח־לִי: וַיֵּלֶךְ וַיִּקַּח וַיָּבֵא לְאִמּוֹ וַתַּעַשׂ אִמּוֹ מַטְעַמִּים כַּאֲשֶׁר אָהֵב אָבִיו: וַתִּקַּח רִבְקָה אֶת־בִּגְדֵי עֵשָׂו בְּנָהּ הַגָּדֹל הַחֲמֻדֹת אֲשֶׁר אִתָּהּ בַּבָּיִת וַתַּלְבֵּשׁ אֶת־יַעֲקֹב בְּנָהּ הַקָּטָן: וְאֵת עֹרֹת גְּדָיֵי הָעִזִּים הִלְבִּישָׁה עַל־יָדָיו וְעַל חֶלְקַת צַוָּארָיו: וַתִּתֵּן אֶת־הַמַּטְעַמִּים וְאֶת־הַלֶּחֶם אֲשֶׁר עָשָׂתָה בְּיַד יַעֲקֹב בְּנָהּ: וַיָּבֹא אֶל־אָבִיו וַיֹּאמֶר אָבִי וַיֹּאמֶר הִנֶּנִּי מִי אַתָּה בְּנִי:

Should the parsimonious use of Jacob's name be surprising?

No. It is consistent with biblical usage. The norm would be not to repeat the name of a character when it is obvious who is performing the action. In addition, the absence of Jacob's name as he enters his father's tent likely reflects Jacob's attempt to keep his identity concealed, since he is masquerading as Esau.

Why then does the Torah decide to mention Jacob by name in the very next verse? It is obvious who is speaking!

Jacob said to his father, "I am Esau, your firstborn. I have done as you told me. Please rise, sit and eat of my game so that your soul may bless me." (Genesis 27:19)

וַיֹּאמֶר יַעֲקֹב אֶל־אָבִיו אָנֹכִי עֵשָׂו בְּכֹרֶךָ עָשִׂיתִי כַּאֲשֶׁר דִּבַּרְתָּ אֵלָי קוּם־נָא שְׁבָה וְאָכְלָה מִצֵּידִי בַּעֲבוּר תְּבָרֲכַנִּי נַפְשֶׁךָ:

Further, we may ask, why is the Torah wordy in the above verse, specifying not only that it was Jacob who was speaking but that he was speaking "to his father"? This is obvious, too. To reinforce our question, let us compare Esau's arrival at his father's tent. There are no added introductory words.

It came to pass, when Isaac finished blessing Jacob, and it was that Jacob had just gone out from the presence of his father, Isaac, that Esau, his brother, returned from his hunting. He, too, prepared delicacies and brought [them] to his father. He said to his father, "Let my father rise and eat of the game of his son so that your soul will bless me." Isaac, his father, said to him, "Who are you?" **He said**, "I am your son, your firstborn, Esau." (Genesis 27:30–32)

וַיְהִי כַּאֲשֶׁר כִּלָּה יִצְחָק לְבָרֵךְ אֶת־יַעֲקֹב וַיְהִי אַךְ יָצֹא יָצָא יַעֲקֹב מֵאֵת פְּנֵי יִצְחָק אָבִיו וְעֵשָׂו אָחִיו בָּא מִצֵּידוֹ: וַיַּעַשׂ גַּם־הוּא מַטְעַמִּים וַיָּבֵא לְאָבִיו וַיֹּאמֶר לְאָבִיו יָקֻם אָבִי וְיֹאכַל מִצֵּיד בְּנוֹ בַּעֲבֻר תְּבָרֲכַנִּי נַפְשֶׁךָ: וַיֹּאמֶר לוֹ יִצְחָק אָבִיו מִי־אָתָּה וַיֹּאמֶר אֲנִי בִּנְךָ בְכֹרְךָ עֵשָׂו:

The elongated introduction in verse 19, וַיֹּאמֶר יַעֲקֹב אֶל־אָבִיו, "Jacob said to his father," which announces Jacob's response to Isaac's question, "Who are you, my son?" – reveals Jacob's inner thoughts. He is hesitant to speak falsely. The added words slow down the pace of the reply; we can feel Jacob's dilemma.[1] Esau, in contrast, need not hesitate to identify himself. He answers immediately, "I am your son, your firstborn, Esau." The Torah uses only one word in Hebrew (וַיֹּאמֶר, [he] said) to introduce Esau's response, while for Jacob, four are used.

Let us return to Jacob's conversation with his father. The principles established above will give us a better appreciation of what follows.

Isaac said to his son, "How is it that you were so quick to find it, my son?" He said, "Because God your Lord caused it to happen before me." (Genesis 27:20)

וַיֹּאמֶר יִצְחָק אֶל־בְּנוֹ מַה־זֶּה מִהַרְתָּ לִמְצֹא בְּנִי וַיֹּאמֶר כִּי הִקְרָה יְהוָה אֱלֹהֶיךָ לְפָנָי:

Once again, in the above verse, the Torah uses a wordy introduction to Isaac's question: "Isaac said to his son . . ." Why doesn't the Torah suffice with stating "He said" (which is only one word in Hebrew)? We know who is speaking, and we know Isaac is speaking to one of his sons. Isaac himself calls him בְּנִי, "my son"!

---

1 These thoughts are based on principles confirmed by Nechama Leibowitz (see chapter titled, "A Classic Example: A Gilayon from Nechama Leibowitz on the Binding of Isaac") but were not directly discussed with her on these verses; Professor Uriel Simon first acquainted me with the literary tool of "retarded motion."

Despite the declaration of the son standing before him, Isaac is uncertain. The person speaking is more refined in his speech than Esau. Therefore, Isaac speaks hesitantly as he ponders the events that he can hear but not see. Without hesitation, Jacob offers a response: "Because the Lord, your God, caused it to happen before me."[2]

Read carefully the verses that follow:

Isaac said to Jacob, "Please come close so that I may feel you, my son, [and confirm] whether you are indeed my son Esau or not." Jacob moved close to Isaac, his father, and he felt him, saying, "The voice is the voice of Jacob but the hands are the hands of Esau." (Genesis 27:21–22)	וַיֹּאמֶר יִצְחָק אֶל־יַעֲקֹב גְּשָׁה־נָּא וַאֲמֻשְׁךָ בְּנִי הַאַתָּה זֶה בְּנִי עֵשָׂו אִם־לֹא: וַיִּגַּשׁ יַעֲקֹב אֶל־יִצְחָק אָבִיו וַיְמֻשֵּׁהוּ וַיֹּאמֶר הַקֹּל קוֹל יַעֲקֹב וְהַיָּדַיִם יְדֵי עֵשָׂו:

The longer-than-usual introduction reflects Isaac's hesitancy. He has significant doubts as to whether or not he is being deceived. Significantly, the Torah's introduction says, "Isaac said to Jacob" rather than "to his son" or "to Esau." Isaac has a strong sense that the one standing before him is his younger son. He asks his son to approach him so that he may touch him and determine which one he is. Jacob is nervous. The Torah shows us how hesitant he is as, once again, it uses a wordy introductory phrase: "Jacob moved close to Isaac, his father, and he felt him." Why not simply say, "He moved closer to him"? In Hebrew, this would be two words, וַיִּגַּשׁ אֵלָיו.[3]

Even after the physical contact, Isaac remains unsure. Nevertheless, he blesses Jacob.

He did not recognize him because his hands were hairy like the hands of his brother Esau, and he blessed him. (Genesis 27:23)	וְלֹא הִכִּירוֹ כִּי־הָיוּ יָדָיו כִּידֵי עֵשָׂו אָחִיו שְׂעִרֹת וַיְבָרְכֵהוּ:

---

2 Here, Jacob is able to answer without hesitation as all events can, in some measure, be attributed to God; author's observation.

3 This observation is based on principles confirmed by Nechama Leibowitz but not directly discussed with her.

Apparently, this was a minor blessing, a test. After this blessing, Isaac again asks for the identity of his son:

He said, "Is it you, my son Esau?" He said, "I am." (Genesis 27:24)

וַיֹּאמֶר אַתָּה זֶה בְּנִי עֵשָׂו וַיֹּאמֶר אָנִי:

Isaac asks quickly. Jacob, now deep into his masquerade and needing to protect his identity, responds without hesitation.[4] Isaac then shares a more elaborate blessing with his son. However, when Esau appears, asking for the blessing that he had been promised, Isaac is confused and hesitant once more. The Torah conveys these feelings via another long introductory phrase:

Isaac, his father, said to him, "Who are you?" He said, "I am your son, your first born, Esau." (Genesis 27:32)

וַיֹּאמֶר לוֹ יִצְחָק אָבִיו מִי־אָתָּה וַיֹּאמֶר אֲנִי בִּנְךָ בְכֹרְךָ עֵשָׂו:

Isaac knows that another son stands before him. The Torah tells us this by adding the single Hebrew word, אָבִיו, "his father," to its identification of Isaac. Yet at the moment, Isaac does not know which son is before him. Nechama envisioned Isaac asking himself in bewilderment: "What's happening here?" He asks succinctly, but with great emotion, "Who are you?"

The clues of names and added words help us to appreciate the high tension and uncertainty throughout this significant event.

---

4 Observation of the author.

THE VOICE OF JACOB

G ENESIS 27:22 CONTAINS ONE OF THE BEST-KNOWN AND widely used biblical quotes:

The voice is the voice of Jacob, but the hands are the   הַקֹּל קוֹל יַעֲקֹב וְהַיָּדַיִם יְדֵי עֵשָׂו
hands of Esau. (Genesis 27:22)

Isaac, who is nearly blind, announces his confusion as to which of his two sons stands before him – Jacob or Esau? Rashi explains that Isaac took careful notice of the manner in which Jacob used his voice. It was not the actual vocal quality, which rendered it difficult to determine identity, but the content. The son who was asked to hunt the meal did not usually speak as the one who delivered the meal. Isaac asked, "How is it that you were so quick to find it, my son?" The response, "Because the Lord your God arranged it for me" (Genesis 27:20), was typical of Jacob, not Esau.

Yet why does Rashi pursue a figurative route? Could it not be that the aged father was referring to the actual sound of his son's voice? After all, voice is one of the means of recognition. A husband and wife may lie with one another at night, even if they have not been able to see one another; they may recognize each other by voice. Why not explain that Isaac detected the voice to sound like Jacob, yet the one in his presence both claimed to be and felt like Esau?

From class, Beit Midrash L'Torah 5733/1973 and correspondence with Nechama Leibowitz
1 Shevat 5752/January 6, 1992.

The Siftei Hahamim offers two defenses of Rashi's opinion. In his first explanation, the Siftei Hahamim states that had the voice, and not the content, been the focus of scrutiny, Isaac should have expressed uncertainty immediately after Jacob first spoke. However, note the flow of the conversation below. (Jacob's initial statements are highlighted.)

He went, he took and he brought [them] to his mother; his mother prepared delicacies, such as his father liked. Rebecca took the costly garments of Esau, her elder son, which were with her in the house, and she dressed Jacob, her younger son. And the hides of the kids she put on his hands and on the smoothness of his neck. She gave the delicacies and the bread that she had prepared into the hand of Jacob her son. He came to his father and said, "**My father!**" He [Isaac] said, "Here I am. Who are you, my son?" Jacob said to his father, "**I am Esau, your firstborn. I have done as you told me. Please rise, sit down and eat of my game, so that your soul may bless me.**" (Genesis 27:14-19)	וַיֵּלֶךְ וַיִּקַּח וַיָּבֵא לְאִמּוֹ וַתַּעַשׂ אִמּוֹ מַטְעַמִּים כַּאֲשֶׁר אָהֵב אָבִיו: וַתִּקַּח רִבְקָה אֶת־בִּגְדֵי עֵשָׂו בְּנָהּ הַגָּדֹל הַחֲמֻדֹת אֲשֶׁר אִתָּהּ בַּבָּיִת וַתַּלְבֵּשׁ אֶת־יַעֲקֹב בְּנָהּ הַקָּטָן: וְאֵת עֹרֹת גְּדָיֵי הָעִזִּים הִלְבִּישָׁה עַל־יָדָיו וְעַל חֶלְקַת צַוָּארָיו: וַתִּתֵּן אֶת־הַמַּטְעַמִּים וְאֶת־הַלֶּחֶם אֲשֶׁר עָשָׂתָה בְּיַד יַעֲקֹב בְּנָהּ: וַיָּבֹא אֶל־אָבִיו וַיֹּאמֶר אָבִי וַיֹּאמֶר הִנֶּנִּי מִי אַתָּה בְּנִי: וַיֹּאמֶר יַעֲקֹב אֶל־אָבִיו אָנֹכִי עֵשָׂו בְּכֹרֶךָ עָשִׂיתִי כַּאֲשֶׁר דִּבַּרְתָּ אֵלָי קוּם־נָא שְׁבָה וְאָכְלָה מִצֵּידִי בַּעֲבוּר תְּבָרֲכַנִּי נַפְשֶׁךָ:

Isaac does not explicitly question his son's identity until Jacob's response to his next question. Then, his uncertainty increases:

The question:

Isaac said to his son, "How is it that you have found [it] so quickly, my son?"	וַיֹּאמֶר יִצְחָק אֶל בְּנוֹ מַה־זֶּה מִהַרְתָּ לִמְצֹא בְּנִי

The answer:

He said, "Because the Lord your God prepared it before me."	וַיֹּאמֶר כִּי הִקְרָה יְהֹוָה אֱ-לֹהֶיךָ לְפָנָי

The response:

Isaac said to Jacob, "Please come closer so that I may feel you, my son, whether you are really my son Esau or not."	וַיֹּאמֶר יִצְחָק אֶל יַעֲקֹב גְּשָׁה נָּא וַאֲמֻשְׁךָ בְּנִי הַאַתָּה זֶה בְּנִי עֵשָׂו אִם לֹא:

The actions:

So Jacob drew near to Isaac, his father, and he felt him, and he said, "The voice is the voice of Jacob, but the hands are the hands of Esau." (Genesis 27:20-22)	וַיִּגַּשׁ יַעֲקֹב אֶל יִצְחָק אָבִיו וַיְמֻשֵּׁהוּ וַיֹּאמֶר הַקֹּל קֹול יַעֲקֹב וְהַיָּדַיִם יְדֵי עֵשָׂו:

From the quality of the voice alone, Isaac could not be sure which of his sons was speaking. Only after Jacob said that God had helped him did Isaac's doubts grow great enough for him to question his son's identity. The statements that he had just heard were not typical of Esau.

Nechama Leibowitz preferred the second explanation of the Siftei Hahamim, which examines the subterfuge from Jacob's perspective:

Jacob told his mother, "But my brother Esau is a hairy man and I am a smooth-skinned man. Perhaps my father will feel me and I shall be as a misleader in his eyes, and I will bring upon myself a curse instead of a blessing." (Genesis 27:11-12)	וַיֹּאמֶר יַעֲקֹב אֶל רִבְקָה אִמּוֹ הֵן עֵשָׂו אָחִי אִישׁ שָׂעִר וְאָנֹכִי אִישׁ חָלָק: אוּלַי יְמֻשֵּׁנִי אָבִי וְהָיִיתִי בְעֵינָיו כִּמְתַעְתֵּעַ וְהֵבֵאתִי עָלַי קְלָלָה וְלֹא בְרָכָה:

Jacob, reacting to his mother's suggestion of the masquerade, was not concerned that his voice would reveal his identity. Apparently, the twin brothers had similar voices. From the sounds of their words alone, it would not be obvious which brother was speaking. Hence Rashi understands Isaac's comment, "The voice is the voice of Jacob, but the hands are the hands of Esau," as referring to the manner of speech that usually distinguished Jacob from Esau.

THE BUD VASE AND USE OF PROPER NAMES IN THE BIBLICAL TEXT

MODESTY WAS A PERVASIVE TRAIT OF NECHAMA LEIBOWITZ. Her speech, dress and living quarters reflected her humble attitude toward life. The walls of her apartment were lined with *sefarim* (books) and the *gilyonot* (study sheets) that she issued for thirty years. I glanced at her collection of Jewish books, trying to identify volumes not yet in her collection that I might buy her as a gift. As I was leaving her apartment that day in the summer of 1993, I showed Nechama a volume of the Torat Haim edition of Humash that I had in my suitcase. Nechama looked at it, told me she did not have it and, perhaps sensing my intention, commented that she had no more space for books. I was disappointed.

I realized it would be difficult to find a gift that would be appropriate for a woman who sought no favors for the Torah she willingly shared. Nevertheless, I wanted to express my gratitude to the one who had equipped me with advanced learning tools and inspired in me a deeper love for the study of Torah. I decided on a silver bud vase. It was small enough not to occupy too much space in her apartment, it was modestly elegant and it was connected to the Torah insight, presented below, that she taught me during one of my visits in December 1990.

When does the Torah use proper names, and when does it omit them? Read the passage below that describes the meeting of Jacob and Esau, the

From conversations with Nechama Leibowitz on 2 Kislev 5751/November 18, 1990 and 13 Elul 5753/August 29, 1993.

first in over twenty years. How often are Jacob and Esau referred to by name?

1. **Jacob lifted** his eyes and saw, and behold, Esau was coming, and with him were four hundred men; so **he divided** the children with Leah and with Rachel and with the two maidservants.

(א) וַיִּשָּׂ֨א יַעֲקֹ֜ב עֵינָ֗יו וַיַּ֙רְא֙ וְהִנֵּ֣ה עֵשָׂ֣ו בָּ֔א וְעִמּ֖וֹ אַרְבַּ֣ע מֵא֣וֹת אִ֑ישׁ וַיַּ֣חַץ אֶת־הַיְלָדִ֗ים עַל־לֵאָה֙ וְעַל־רָחֵ֔ל וְעַ֖ל שְׁתֵּ֥י הַשְּׁפָחֽוֹת:

2. **He placed** the maidservants and their children first and Leah and her children after, and Rachel and Joseph last.

(ב) וַיָּ֧שֶׂם אֶת־הַשְּׁפָח֛וֹת וְאֶת־יַלְדֵיהֶ֖ן רִֽאשֹׁנָ֑ה וְאֶת־לֵאָ֤ה וִֽילָדֶ֙יהָ֙ אַחֲרֹנִ֔ים וְאֶת־רָחֵ֥ל וְאֶת־יוֹסֵ֖ף אַחֲרֹנִֽים:

3. **He went** ahead of them and **prostrated himself** to the ground seven times, until **he came** close to his brother.

(ג) וְה֖וּא עָבַ֣ר לִפְנֵיהֶ֑ם וַיִּשְׁתַּ֤חוּ אַ֙רְצָה֙ שֶׁ֣בַע פְּעָמִ֔ים עַד־גִּשְׁתּ֖וֹ עַד־אָחִֽיו:

4. **Esau ran** toward him and **embraced** him, and **he fell** on his neck and **kissed** him, and **they wept**.

(ד) וַיָּ֨רׇץ עֵשָׂ֤ו לִקְרָאתוֹ֙ וַֽיְחַבְּקֵ֔הוּ וַיִּפֹּ֥ל עַל־צַוָּארָ֖ו וַֽיִּשָּׁקֵ֑הוּ וַיִּבְכּֽוּ:

5. **He lifted** his eyes and **saw** the women and the children, and **he said**, "Who are these to you?" **He said**, "The children with whom God has favored your servant."

(ה) וַיִּשָּׂ֣א אֶת־עֵינָ֗יו וַיַּ֤רְא אֶת־הַנָּשִׁים֙ וְאֶת־הַיְלָדִ֔ים וַיֹּ֖אמֶר מִי־אֵ֣לֶּה לָּ֑ךְ וַיֹּאמַ֕ר הַיְלָדִ֕ים אֲשֶׁר־חָנַ֥ן אֱלֹהִ֖ים אֶת־עַבְדֶּֽךָ:

6. The maidservants and their children drew near and prostrated themselves.

(ו) וַתִּגַּ֣שְׁןָ הַשְּׁפָח֗וֹת הֵ֛נָּה וְיַלְדֵיהֶ֖ן וַתִּֽשְׁתַּחֲוֶֽיןָ:

7. And Leah and her children drew near and prostrated themselves, and after [them], Joseph and Rachel drew near and prostrated themselves.

(ז) וַתִּגַּ֧שׁ גַּם־לֵאָ֛ה וִילָדֶ֖יהָ וַיִּֽשְׁתַּחֲו֑וּ וְאַחַ֗ר נִגַּ֥שׁ יוֹסֵ֛ף וְרָחֵ֖ל וַיִּֽשְׁתַּחֲוֽוּ:

8. **He said**, "What is to you [the purpose of] all this camp that I have met?" **He said**, "To find favor in my master's eyes."

(ח) וַיֹּ֕אמֶר מִ֥י לְךָ֛ כׇּל־הַמַּחֲנֶ֥ה הַזֶּ֖ה אֲשֶׁ֣ר פָּגָ֑שְׁתִּי וַיֹּ֕אמֶר לִמְצֹא־חֵ֖ן בְּעֵינֵ֥י אֲדֹנִֽי:

9. **Esau said**, "I have plenty, my brother; let what you have remain yours."

(ט) וַיֹּ֥אמֶר עֵשָׂ֖ו יֶשׁ־לִ֣י רָ֑ב אָחִ֕י יְהִ֥י לְךָ֖ אֲשֶׁר־לָֽךְ:

10. **Jacob said**, "Please, no! If indeed I have found favor in your eyes, then you shall take my gift from my hand, because I have seen your face, which is like seeing the face of an angel, and you have accepted me.

(י) וַיֹּ֣אמֶר יַעֲקֹ֗ב אַל־נָא֙ אִם־נָ֨א מָצָ֤אתִי חֵן֙ בְּעֵינֶ֔יךָ וְלָקַחְתָּ֥ מִנְחָתִ֖י מִיָּדִ֑י כִּ֣י עַל־כֵּ֞ן רָאִ֣יתִי פָנֶ֗יךָ כִּרְאֹ֛ת פְּנֵ֥י אֱלֹהִ֖ים וַתִּרְצֵֽנִי:

11. Now take my gift, which has been brought to you, for God has favored me [with it], and [because] I have everything." **He prevailed** upon him, and he **took** [it]. (Genesis Chapter 33:1-11)

(יא) קַח־נָא אֶת־בִּרְכָתִי אֲשֶׁר הֻבָאת לָךְ כִּי־חַנַּנִי אֱ־לֹהִים וְכִי יֶשׁ־לִי־כֹל וַיִּפְצַר־בּוֹ וַיִּקָּח:

In the biblical text, the first time a character is introduced in an active role, his name is (usually) recorded. In subsequent verses, the pattern (in Hebrew) is to record the verb alone. (As the Hebrew verb is automatically conjugated according to person and gender, the English translation for each verb is comprised of the action and a pronoun representing the one performing the activity.) Nechama Leibowitz posited that once the character has been identified, there is no need to repeat his identity as long as it is clear who is the subject or object of any given verb. Notice how, in our selection, even verse 4, which could be somewhat ambiguous in its middle and final sections, relies only on the first mention of Esau's name. Verse 5, which includes three actions by Esau and one by Jacob, records no names because the reader is able to discern who performs which action.

Why then is Esau's name recorded in verse 9 when it is obvious who is speaking? The boastful statement, יֶשׁ־לִי רָב, "I have plenty," explained Nechama, is a defining one, reflecting the nature and attitude of Esau. As such, the Torah associates the name of the subject to clearly identify Esau's personality. The Torah then records Jacob's name in the succeeding verse to contrast the personalities.

Nechama Leibowitz noted the contrast between Jacob's gift to Esau and the gift that he had his sons offer the viceroy of Egypt (see Genesis 43:11). Fearing for his children's safety, painfully aware that one son was held captive in Egypt and concerned that all his children would be accused of stealing back the money they had paid for grain, Jacob instructed his children to bring "a bit of balsam, a bit of honey, wax, lotus, pistachios and almonds" as an offering to the Egyptian leader. This was a modest presentation to the viceroy of the most powerful country in the ancient world. Why was this gift so different from the one that Jacob sent to Esau?

When Nechama Leibowitz taught this segment to a group of high-school girls, one of the pupils suggested that the two encounters might be compared to two gentlemen courting their ladies. One brings a basket of flowers, while the other brings two long-stemmed roses. While one gift is large in quantity, the other is lovelier and more appropriate. Jacob's children present the Egyptian ruler with a symbolic and lovely gift. Jacob, in recognition of Esau's nature and perhaps in an effort to compensate for the blessing Esau felt should have been his, offers a large gift. Esau is impressed by quantity and boasts of it. In contrast, Jacob answers, יֶשׁ־לִי־כֹל – "I have everything." By doing so, he exemplifies the teaching of our sages of blessed memory:

Who is wealthy? The one who is satisfied with his portion. (Avot 4:1)   אֵיזֶהוּ עָשִׁיר? הַשָּׂמֵחַ בְּחֶלְקוֹ.

In an attempt to convince Nechama Leibowitz to accept my gift, I reminded her of the lesson that she had taught me. I asked that she allow my gift to be a symbol of the Torah that she had given me. The vase stands in my display case at home. Nechama had no interest in another worldly possession.

A Psak from Rav Shlomo Zalman Auerbach zt"l

NECHAMA LEIBOWITZ LIVED IN JERUSALEM'S KIRYAT MOSHE neighborhood. In order to reach the synagogue where she prayed on Shabbat, she walked past the Tel Aviv–Jerusalem highway. Frequently, drivers would stop to ask her for directions. Nechama ignored them, fearing that answering them would be a violation of the prohibition against enabling others to sin. One of Nechama's students suggested that she ask for a rabbinic decision on the issue. Although Nechama was reluctant at first, in the end she agreed to allow the student to ask Rav Shlomo Zalman Auerbach on her behalf.

Rabbi Auerbach ruled that Nechama should answer drivers who asked for directions on Shabbat for two reasons. The first was that if she did not answer, the drivers might commit additional violations if they chose the wrong way to travel. The second reason was that not answering might create animosity (*evah*), and it was very important to avoid this type of discord between Jews.

From conversation with Nechama Leibowitz on 5 Elul 5753/August 21, 1993.

RICHES FROM EGYPT

Appropriate or Appropriated?

AS GOD PREPARES THE WAY FOR THE EXODUS FROM EGYPT, HE directs Moses to command the Jews to take gold and silver vessels from the Egyptians. Why were these riches taken? Were they gifts to the Jews from the Egyptians or were they given on loan? If the Egyptians complied with the Jews' request on the premise that they were given on loan, would our ancestors, under the direction of God and Moses, be guilty of deception? After all, we had no intention of returning to Egypt, nor would we be shipping the items back to their owners.

The Torah (Exodus 11:2) states:

Please speak into the ears of the people, and let them ask, each man from his friend and each woman from her friend, silver vessels and golden vessels.	דַּבֶּר־נָא בְּאָזְנֵי הָעָם וְיִשְׁאֲלוּ אִישׁ מֵאֵת רֵעֵהוּ וְאִשָּׁה מֵאֵת רְעוּתָהּ כְּלֵי־כֶסֶף וּכְלֵי זָהָב.

There are some commentators who understand the word "ask" as meaning "to borrow."

Nechama Leibowitz was emphatic in her rejection of this translation and of the idea that the Jews practiced any deception upon leaving Egypt. She noted that Hebrew is often more limited in its vocabulary than English. In English, we find root words taking on multiple and sometimes very

---

From conversations with Nechama Leibowitz on 1 Iyar 5753/April 22, 1993 and 3 Sivan 5753/May 23, 1993.

different meanings by the addition of prefixes. In Hebrew, there is no prefix of this nature. But a Hebrew word's meaning may be altered by associative words and prefixes used in these associative words. For example, לְקַנֵּא בִּפְלוֹנִי means to be envious of Peloni. But לְקַנֵּא לִפְלוֹנִי means to be zealous on Peloni's behalf.

There is an example in the Torah where the root word שאל means to borrow. In discussing personal liability for the property of others, the Torah states:

If a person should borrow [an animal] from his neighbor and it breaks a limb or dies, if its owner is not with him, he shall surely pay. (Exodus 22:13)	וְכִי יִשְׁאַל אִישׁ מֵעִם רֵעֵהוּ וְנִשְׁבַּר אוֹ מֵת בְּעָלָיו אֵין עִמּוֹ שַׁלֵּם יְשַׁלֵּם.

Note that the word שאל is used in conjunction with מֵעִם. The combination of words means "to borrow," as is obvious from the context of the verse. However, the verse containing the command to take vessels from the Egyptians says וְיִשְׁאֲלוּ ... מֵאֵת. This usage means to ask for an outright gift. This opinion is supported by the Rashbam (see 3:22 and 11:2) the Hizkuni, Rabbenu Hananel and others.

To explain the Rashbam's position further, I add the observation that the word "et" (אֶת) usually has no translation but is used before a direct object. However, at times it means "with," as we find in Genesis 13:5:

Also Lot, who went with Abram, had flocks, cattle and tents.	וְגַם־לְלוֹט הַהֹלֵךְ אֶת־אַבְרָם הָיָה צֹאן־וּבָקָר וְאֹהָלִים.

The degree of bonding reflected by the word "et" (אֶת) is not as close as the bond that is indicated by the word "im" (עִם). This nuance enables us to understand God's anger with Bilam in the narrative recorded in chapter 22 of the Book of Numbers. Although God allows Bilam to accompany the messengers from Moab (Numbers 22:20), He expresses anger when Bilam sets out. Why?

A careful reading of the text reveals that God permitted לֵךְ אִתָּם [go with ("et") them], which implies a casual connection. However, Bilam supports Moab's goal of cursing the Jews, as is reflected in the Torah's description:

וַיֵּלֶךְ עִם־שָׂרֵי מוֹאָב [he went with ("im") the officers of Moab]. "Im" implies a close association. Similarly, when it is used together with יִשְׁאַל (Exodus 22:13) it conveys the fact that the ownership remains with the original party while the object has only been lent. From this, we see that the silver and gold vessels were to be taken, וְיִשְׁאֲלוּ ... מֵאֵת, not borrowed.

It is strange that God gives the command to Moses in the form of a request:

| Please speak into the ears of the people and let them ask, each man from his friend and each woman from her friend, silver vessels and golden vessels.[1] | דַּבֶּר־נָא בְּאָזְנֵי הָעָם וְיִשְׁאֲלוּ אִישׁ מֵאֵת רֵעֵהוּ וְאִשָּׁה מֵאֵת רְעוּתָהּ כְּלֵי־כֶסֶף וּכְלֵי זָהָב. |

As Rashi implies, God speaks to Moses, who is attuned to the mood of the nation, saying: I know that the people are eager for their freedom and willing to forego this opportunity to accumulate material wealth. But I am not willing to abandon My plan. Please speak with them and convince them to ask for the gold and silver vessels and the clothing.

Why was it so important to God that the Israelites collect these riches?

Nechama suggested that justice serves as one basis for the Divine decision. For decades, the Jews had labored for the Egyptians without compensation. Now, they would receive it in a lump sum. But this payment was also intended to be instructive for future generations. Just as God provided the material resources to help the Jewish nation start to build a new life, so too would Jews be commanded to provide a *haanakah* – a generous grant – to the Jewish indentured servant upon his release from service.[2] As this individual begins to reintegrate himself into society and provide for his daily needs, the Jew who benefited from his labor must help him become established. God modeled the behavior He expects from His people in order to implant this value in us. We must assume social responsibility for others.

---

1 Rashi translates נא as "please." The view of the Ibn Ezra is that the word means "now." Nechama shared with me that while נא – which is an abbreviated form of אנא – can mean "now" on occasion, its usual definition is "please." Nechama felt strongly that in our context, the word follows its usual meaning of "please."

2 See Rashi on Deuteronomy 15:15.

I shared with Nechama Rabbi Joseph Soloveitchik's elaboration on the same question. The Rav noted that the Torah contains four references to the taking of riches. The first one is in Abraham's time.

He said to Abram, "You shall surely know that your descendants will be strangers in a land that is not theirs; they will enslave them and oppress them for four hundred years. And also the nation that they will serve will I judge, and afterwards they will go forth with great possessions." (Genesis 15:13-14)	וַיֹּאמֶר לְאַבְרָם יָדֹעַ תֵּדַע כִּי־גֵר יִהְיֶה זַרְעֲךָ בְּאֶרֶץ לֹא לָהֶם וַעֲבָדוּם וְעִנּוּ אֹתָם אַרְבַּע מֵאוֹת שָׁנָה: וְגַם אֶת־הַגּוֹי אֲשֶׁר יַעֲבֹדוּ דָּן אָנֹכִי וְאַחֲרֵי־כֵן יֵצְאוּ בִּרְכֻשׁ גָּדוֹל:

Why, when God informed Abraham that his descendants will serve as slaves, was it necessary to add that they would ultimately leave with great wealth? Why, when Moses stood at the burning bush and accepted his mission to lead the Jewish people out of Egypt, was it necessary to tell Moses the Jews would ask for valuables from the Egyptians? This episode at the burning bush took place approximately one full year before the exodus and the directive would be commanded in its proper time!

Rabbi Soloveitchik, who was of the opinion that וְיִשְׁאֲלוּ ... מֵאֵת means to demand, explained that the Jewish people's ability to demand payment for their work was a critical experience in restoring their sense of dignity. Redemption from bondage must include not only physical freedom, but psychological freedom as well. Restored dignity was an essential ingredient in forging the newly liberated slaves into a kingdom of priests. Therefore, while the Israelites did not fully understand the reason for asking the Egyptians for riches, God did. He therefore asked Moses to persuade the people to do so. Nechama held this explanation in high esteem.

When God spoke to Moses at the burning bush and informed him of the taking of the riches, He said:

Each woman shall ask from her neighbor and from the dweller in her house silver and gold objects and garments, and you shall put [them] on your sons and on your daughters, and you shall empty out Egypt. (Exodus 3:22)	וְשָׁאֲלָה אִשָּׁה מִשְּׁכֶנְתָּהּ וּמִגָּרַת בֵּיתָהּ כְּלֵי־כֶסֶף וּכְלֵי זָהָב וּשְׂמָלֹת וְשַׂמְתֶּם עַל־בְּנֵיכֶם וְעַל־בְּנֹתֵיכֶם וְנִצַּלְתֶּם אֶת־מִצְרָיִם:

Just before the exodus, God phrases the command:

Please speak into the ears of the people and let them ask, *each man from his friend and each woman from her friend*, silver vessels and golden vessels. (Exodus 11:2)	דַּבֶּר נָא בְּאָזְנֵי הָעָם וְיִשְׁאֲלוּ אִישׁ מֵאֵת רֵעֵהוּ וְאִשָּׁה מֵאֵת רְעוּתָהּ כְּלֵי־כֶסֶף וּכְלֵי זָהָב.

Why the change? Why does the first specific reference to this process mention only the women's action? In the weekly gilayon for Bo, 5715/1954), Nechama quoted the *Midrash Hemdat Yamim* cited by the *Torah Shelema*. Many Jewish women gave their jewelry to their Egyptian neighbors and Pharaoh's soldiers as bribes to persuade them not to reveal the presence of their newborn sons, so that the babies would not be drowned in the Nile. According to God, this money, which paid for an action that any human being should have done of one's own accord, must not stay in Egypt. God's abhorrence of the Egyptians' act leads God to ascribe a priority status to retrieving this money. As the Jewish women were the ones to pass gold and silver to the Egyptians, they are mentioned first to emphasize the reestablishment of the rightful ownership of these assets.

Perhaps the *Midrash Hemdat Yamim* provides another answer as to why God used the word נָא here. As stated above, God understood that the Jewish people would focus on their impending freedom and be willing to forego the opportunity to collect gold and silver from the Egyptians. But God, not wanting the Egyptian society to benefit from the Israelites' wealth, asks Moses to convince the nation of the importance of taking the riches with them.[3]

---

3 While Rashi's understanding of נָא as "please" makes it clear that God is asking something which would not have been self-assumed by the Jewish nation, it appears the phrase of דַּבֶּר בְּאָזְנֵי does, in itself, convey the intention to convince. We find such usage in the dramatic encounter between Judah and the Egyptian Viceroy (who is actually Joseph). Judah delivers an impassioned plea to be accepted as a slave in place of his brother, Benjamin, accused of stealing the Viceroy's silver goblet. Judah's request to speak (again) is introduced by the following phrase (in Genesis 44:18): יְדַבֶּר-נָא עַבְדְּךָ דָבָר בְּאָזְנֵי אֲדֹנִי (May your servant please speak a word in my master's ear?)

(Observation of author based on comment shared in a Torah discussion with Dr. Michael Paritsky.)

The Rashbam, in his brief commentary on Exodus 3:22, says that the proper understanding of the word שָׁאַל will provide an answer to the heretics who focus on deception. The above development enables the student of Torah to establish that the Israelites' exodus from Egypt was couched in honesty, justice and sensitivity. We received gifts from the Egyptians; some gave us gifts to speed our departure, others out of recognition that they owed us back wages. Our sensitivity to the needs of others, as we continue to travel the path of time, must reflect God's sensitivity to our own needs during the exodus.

O UR SAGES IN THE TALMUD (ZEVAHIM 116A) DEBATE THE DATE
of Jethro's arrival to visit Moses and the Israelites. Rabbi Yehoshua
is of the opinion that Jethro arrived before the Revelation at
Mount Sinai. Indeed, this is the order of events in the Torah. The portion,
named after Moses's father-in-law, Jethro, begins with him, his daughter,
Tziporah, and her two sons arriving at Mount Sinai. The Revelation and
giving of the Ten Commandments are recorded later in the text.

Rabbi Eliezer ha-Modai disagrees. His opinion is that the sequence of
the texts does not reflect the chronological order of events. According to
him, Jethro arrived after the Revelation at Mount Sinai.

The Ramban develops both views. Initially, he cites four proofs supporting the view that the Torah recorded events out of sequence and that
Jethro arrived at the Israelite encampment only after the Revelation. Three
of his proofs follow.

First proof: In recording Jethro's visit, the Torah tells us:

Jethro, Moses's father-in-law, came and his sons,	וַיָּבֹא יִתְרוֹ חֹתֵן מֹשֶׁה וּבָנָיו וְאִשְׁתּוֹ
and his wife to the desert that he was encamping	אֶל־מֹשֶׁה אֶל־הַמִּדְבָּר אֲשֶׁר־הוּא
there, to the Mountain of God. (Exodus 18:5)	חֹנֶה שָׁם הַר הָאֱלֹהִים:

At first glance, the phrase "that he was encamping there" appears unnecessary. Its inclusion alludes to the fact that the nation, which camped at

From conversation with Nechama Leibowitz on 1 Nisan 5753/March 23, 1993.

Mount Sinai for a full year, was already established there, at the Mountain of God, by the time Jethro arrived. They were not present at Mount Sinai before the Revelation.[1, 2]

Second proof: The day after his arrival, Jethro becomes concerned over the routine he observes. Moses is busy from morning to night dealing with issues brought to him by the people. When Jethro questions his son-in-law, Moses replies:

Whenever they have a concern, they come to me.	כִּי־יִהְיֶה לָהֶם דָּבָר בָּא אֵלַי
I must judge between a man and his neighbor; I	וְשָׁפַטְתִּי בֵּין אִישׁ וּבֵין רֵעֵהוּ
must make known to them the statutes of God and	וְהוֹדַעְתִּי אֶת־חֻקֵּי הָאֱלֹהִים
His teachings. (Exodus 18:16)	וְאֶת־תּוֹרֹתָיו׃

What is the source of these statutes and teachings? Revelation at Mount Sinai!

Third proof: When Moses speaks to the Israelites in Deuteronomy 1:6–19, he mentions the nation's departure from Mount Sinai as occurring at the same time that he shared his need for judges to assist him. These appointments resulted from Jethro's advice to Moses. As Jethro's guidance was given the day after his arrival and as the Israelites' departure from Mount Sinai (where they camped for a year) came soon afterwards, it appears certain that Jethro arrived after the Revelation.

If Rabbi Eliezer ha-Modai's opinion is correct, we must find a reason for the Torah's election to record events out of sequence. The Ramban offers the Ibn Ezra's suggestion. The incident that takes place just before the beginning of the Torah portion named after Jethro is the unprovoked attack by Amalek. In its aftermath, God announces His intention to obliterate the Amalekites. By placing Jethro's arrival immediately afterward, the Torah is suggesting that we must be careful to repay good to Jethro just as we will

---

1 Cf. Rabbi Chavel's notation on the Ramban's commentary, Exodus 18:1.

2 While the Israelites arrived several days before the actual Revelation, the Ramban, in citing this proof, appears not to consider these days as a possible window of time for Jethro's arrival. The established stay conveyed by the Torah's reference, "that he was en-camping there," indicates that the nation had already been at Mount Sinai for more than several days.

repay evil to Amalek. (The Kenite nation, which descended from Jethro, lived beside Amalek. When the Israelites, under the future leadership of King Saul, would launch their attack against Amalek, the Torah's juxtaposition of events here will serve as a warning that we must take care not to harm Jethro's descendants.)

As compelling as these proofs may be, the Ramban himself dismisses them. He asks: if Jethro arrived after the Revelation at Mount Sinai, how is it possible that the Torah omitted this monumental event from its list of Jethro's reasons for visiting the Israelites?

The Torah states:

Jethro, the Priest of Midian, father-in-law of Moses, heard all that God had done for Moses and for Israel, his nation, which God took Israel out of Egypt. (Exodus 18:1)	וַיִּשְׁמַע יִתְרוֹ כֹהֵן מִדְיָן חֹתֵן מֹשֶׁה אֵת כָּל־אֲשֶׁר עָשָׂה אֱ-לֹהִים לְמֹשֶׁה וּלְיִשְׂרָאֵל עַמּוֹ כִּי־הוֹצִיא יְ-הֹוָה אֶת־יִשְׂרָאֵל מִמִּצְרָיִם

Had Jethro arrived after the Revelation, a reference to God's appearance at Mount Sinai certainly would have been included in the above verse.[3] The Ramban's conclusion is that the Torah's recorded order matches the chronological order of events. Jethro arrived prior to the giving of the Torah.[4]

In his fourth proof supporting Rabbi Eliezer ha-Modai's position, and the one not cited above, the Ramban introduces a multi-dimensional topic. Twice, the Torah records Jethro's return, or attempted return, to his homeland. The first reference follows Moses's implementation of Jethro's plan for a judicial system:

---

3 The Ramban offers an answer, which essentially is a hybrid position. He entertains the possibility that Jethro begins his journey to join Moses and the Jewish people after hearing about the wonders of the exodus, as stated by the opening verse of the Torah portion named Yitro. However, Jethro does not reach the encampment at Mount Sinai until after the Revelation.

4 The Ramban's general position is to acknowledge the Torah's accounts as having been recorded in chronological order.

Moses took his father-in-law's advice and did all that he said. Moses chose capable men from all of Israel and appointed them heads of the people, leaders of thousands, leaders of hundreds, leaders of fifties and leaders of tens. They judged the people at all times; the difficult cases they would bring to Moses, and all of the simple cases they would adjudicate. Moses sent off his father-in-law, and he went to his homeland. (Exodus 18:24–27)

וַיִּשְׁמַע מֹשֶׁה לְקוֹל חֹתְנוֹ וַיַּעַשׂ כֹּל אֲשֶׁר אָמָר: וַיִּבְחַר מֹשֶׁה אַנְשֵׁי־חַיִל מִכָּל־יִשְׂרָאֵל וַיִּתֵּן אֹתָם רָאשִׁים עַל־הָעָם שָׂרֵי אֲלָפִים שָׂרֵי מֵאוֹת שָׂרֵי חֲמִשִּׁים וְשָׂרֵי עֲשָׂרֹת: וְשָׁפְטוּ אֶת־הָעָם בְּכָל־עֵת אֶת־הַדָּבָר הַקָּשֶׁה יְבִיאוּן אֶל־מֹשֶׁה וְכָל־הַדָּבָר הַקָּטֹן יִשְׁפּוּטוּ הֵם: וַיְשַׁלַּח מֹשֶׁה אֶת־חֹתְנוֹ וַיֵּלֶךְ לוֹ אֶל־אַרְצוֹ:

The second reference to Jethro's intended departure from the Israelite encampment is found much later in the Torah; it is in the Book of Numbers (10:29–30). There, we find the dialogue presented below, which occurred approximately one year after the Revelation:

Moses said to Hovav the son of Reuel the Midianite, father-in-law of Moses, "We are journeying to the place of which God has said, 'I shall give it to you.' Go with us and we shall do good to you, for God has spoken of good for Israel."

וַיֹּאמֶר מֹשֶׁה לְחֹבָב בֶּן־רְעוּאֵל הַמִּדְיָנִי חֹתֵן מֹשֶׁה נֹסְעִים אֲנַחְנוּ אֶל־הַמָּקוֹם אֲשֶׁר אָמַר יְהֹוָה אֹתוֹ אֶתֵּן לָכֶם לְכָה אִתָּנוּ וְהֵטַבְנוּ לָךְ כִּי־יְהֹוָה דִּבֶּר־טוֹב עַל־יִשְׂרָאֵל:

Jethro answers:

He said to him, "I will not go. Rather, to my land and to my family I shall go."

וַיֹּאמֶר אֵלָיו לֹא אֵלֵךְ כִּי אִם־אֶל־אַרְצִי וְאֶל־מוֹלַדְתִּי אֵלֵךְ:

Moses does not wish to accept this. He persists:

He [Moses] said, "Please do not abandon us, for after all, you know the places we are going to camp in the desert and you can be our guide. And it shall be that if you go with us, it shall be that the good God does with us, we will do with you." They journeyed

וַיֹּאמֶר אַל־נָא תַּעֲזֹב אֹתָנוּ כִּי עַל־כֵּן יָדַעְתָּ חֲנֹתֵנוּ בַּמִּדְבָּר וְהָיִיתָ לָּנוּ לְעֵינָיִם: וְהָיָה כִּי־תֵלֵךְ עִמָּנוּ וְהָיָה הַטּוֹב הַהוּא אֲשֶׁר יֵיטִיב יְהֹוָה עִמָּנוּ וְהֵטַבְנוּ לָךְ: וַיִּסְעוּ מֵהַר

from the Mountain of God a three-day distance, and the Ark of the Covenant of God traveled before them at a three-day distance to scout out for them a resting place. (Numbers 10:31–33)

יְהֹוָה דֶּרֶךְ שְׁלֹשֶׁת יָמִים וַאֲרוֹן בְּרִית־יְהֹוָה נֹסֵעַ לִפְנֵיהֶם דֶּרֶךְ שְׁלֹשֶׁת יָמִים לָתוּר לָהֶם מְנוּחָה:

The Torah does not state definitively whether Jethro acceded to Moses's plea and joined the Israelites on their journey or not. Rashi holds he did not. In fact, according to Rashi, the verses describing Jethro's visit recorded earlier in Exodus and the verses describing Moses's request to his father-in-law to join the Jewish nation in their journey to the Promised Land refer to the same episode. Jethro made only one trip to the Israelites (Rashi appears to hold that Jethro came after the Revelation[5]), but the story is chronicled in two different portions in the Torah. Sometime after Moses took his father-in-law's advice and put it into effect, Jethro returns to his homeland. To Rashi, Jethro has a new mission: to bring the word of God to his family.[6]

The Ramban believes that Jethro made two separate visits to the Jewish encampment. His first visit took place before the Revelation. After the giving of the Ten Commandments and Jethro's advice about appointing assistants to judge the people, Moses sends Jethro, who is eager to return to Midian and guide his family's conversion to the Israelite faith, back to his home. Then, having completed his mission, Jethro rejoins the Jewish nation and accompanies them on their journeys. (The Ramban understands the absence of a response to Moses's second request to stay with the Jewish people as an indication that this time, Jethro agreed.)

---

5 See Rashi 18:9, "all the good." Rashi elaborates, explaining that Jethro was moved by the giving of the manna, the well of water and the Torah. See also Rashi on verse 13.

6 The word וַיְשַׁלַּח is distinct from וַיְשַׁלֵּח . While the Hebrew letters are the same, the vocalization indicates that they are two different forms of a shared root word.

וַיְשַׁלֵּח means to send on a mission. וַיְשַׁלַּח means to send off (without the sender providing a task for the traveler), to let go (as in שַׁלַּח אֶת־עַמִּי, let My people go) or to escort. As I understand Rashi's position, Moses's plea to Jethro אַל־נָא תַּעֲזֹב אֹתָנוּ – please do not abandon us – caused Jethro to hesitate to return to his homeland. When Moses accepted that he could not persuade Jethro to stay, Moses let him go on his way – hence the use of the word וַיְשַׁלַּח. Jethro returned to his family and never rejoined the Jewish people. However, his descendants joined the Jewish nation in the Promised Land.

While Nechama Leibowitz understood the arguments of both schools of thought, she favored Rashi's view that Jethro went to the Israelite encampment only once. If so, I noted, we must question the placement of the following verse:

Moses sent off his father-in-law, and he went to his homeland. (Exodus 18:27)   וַיְשַׁלַּח מֹשֶׁה אֶת־חֹתְנוֹ וַיֵּלֶךְ לוֹ אֶל־אַרְצוֹ׃

Why does the Torah refer to Jethro's final decision when we are only in the middle of the story? Should not the Torah have saved this statement for the dialogue presented later, in the Torah portion named Be-ha'alotcha? Would it not have been a fitting conclusion to Moses's father-in-law's sole visit?

Why does Jethro come to visit Moses and the Israelites? He is excited about the reports he heard regarding the exodus and the many other wonders that God performed. Once Jethro arrives at the Israelite encampment, he learns more from Moses, and develops a deeper appreciation of God's power and the beauty of His word. These experiences motivate Jethro to share his new spiritual insights with his family back in Midian.

I suggested to Nechama that because Jethro's desire to return to his family stemmed from the encounter described earlier in Exodus, the Torah mentions the end of the story up front. This literary device reveals that Jethro left the Israelite encampment not because he was tired of his new surroundings or because he was homesick. Rather, the Torah captures Jethro's excitement and desire to invite others to share in the recognition and acceptance of God's greatness. Jethro made his decision not at the visit's end, but at its beginning, when he synthesized his own knowledge with the greater knowledge that Moses provided him. Nechama answered, "A plausible explanation. Very nice."

Love Thy Neighbor

Who Is He?

T HE DICTUM IS ONE OF THE MOST WELL KNOWN OF THE TORAH'S commandments:

Love thy neighbor as thyself. (Leviticus 19:18)   וְאָהַבְתָּ לְרֵעֲךָ כָּמוֹךָ

Who is our neighbor? Who is included in this major Torah principle?

While most authorities restrict this high level obligation to members of the Jewish faith, Nechama said that the Exodus narrative demonstrated otherwise.

God commands Moses:

Please speak into the ears of the people and let them   דַּבֶּר־נָא בְּאָזְנֵי הָעָם וְיִשְׁאֲלוּ אִישׁ
ask, each man from his neighbor and each woman   מֵאֵת רֵעֵהוּ וְאִשָּׁה־מֵאֵת רְעוּתָהּ
from her neighbor, silver vessels and golden vessels.   כְּלֵי־כֶסֶף וּכְלֵי זָהָב:
(Exodus 11:2)

The word רֵעֵהוּ – "his friend/neighbor" in the verse cited above – is a clear reference to the Egyptians. רֵעַ (friend/neighbor) means someone who is near you. So, too, the word must be understood in the command to love one's neighbor as oneself. It applies, Nechama said, to all people.

This view is presented in, and may likely be based on, the commentary

---

From conversation with Nechama Leibowitz on 3 Sivan 5753/May 23, 1993.

of Rabbi David Tzvi Hoffman, whom Nechama Leibowitz frequently quoted. Rabbi Hoffman acknowledges that, at times, the word רֵעַ can refer to another Jew. However, he bids us to look at the complete verse:

You shall neither take revenge nor bear a grudge against the members of your nation. You shall love your neighbor as yourself: I am the Lord. (Leviticus 19:18)	לֹא־תִקֹּם וְלֹא־תִטֹּר אֶת־בְּנֵי עַמֶּךָ וְאָהַבְתָּ לְרֵעֲךָ כָּמוֹךָ אֲנִי יְ־הוָה:

Note that in the very same verse the expression בְּנֵי עַמֶּךָ, members of your nation, is used to limit the law to members of the Jewish faith. In the verse immediately preceding ours the Jews are referred to as עֲמִיתֶךָ, also based on the word עַם, nation. The fact that the Torah switches terms to רֵעַ, signals that in this context, רֵעַ means all people.

This view appears to also be advanced by the *Ha-Ketav ve-ha-Kabbalah*. Commenting on the phrase וְאָהַבְתָּ לְרֵעֲךָ כָּמוֹךָ – "Love thy neighbor as thyself" – the author says, "All manner of good and kindness that a person accepts in his mind and heart as appropriate for himself to receive from his friend, he should do for his neighbor, which is every person."

A TIME TO REBUKE, A TIME TO PROVIDE

Reflections on Moses's Sin

D ESPITE REPEATED PRAYERS, MOSES WAS DENIED ENTRY TO the Land of Israel. As most commentators explain, his sin took place at the Waters of Meriva, when he struck the rock in order to produce water (Numbers 20:11). While the scene of Moses's sin has received nearly universal consensus, its precise nature has eluded explanation.

Nechama Leibowitz cited the Shadal (Numbers 20:12) to illustrate the results of this lack of clarity: "Moses, our Master, committed one sin, and the commentators piled on him thirteen transgressions or more! Each of them invented a new sin, so I have refrained from a thorough exploration of this topic for fear that I might produce a new opinion and find myself, also, adding another sin onto Moses, our Master."

The most recognized explanation of the transgression is that of the *Midrash Tanhuma*, which has been popularized by Rashi: although Moses was commanded to speak to the rock, he struck it instead. The Ramban challenges this view. He notes that God ordered Moses to take his staff in his hand. It was the same staff Moses used to strike the rock, according to God's command, at the nation's earlier encampment at Refidim (later to be renamed Masa u-Meriva). Had God's intention not been for Moses to strike the rock, why tell Moses to take it up? Rather, says the Ramban, it was understood that Moses would follow the same procedure that he did at Masa u-Meriva, the first time water came from a rock, as we read:

From gilyonot Hukat 5718 (1958), 5729 (1969), and correspondence dated Tammuz 5752/ July 1992.

Behold, I will stand before you there at the rock in Horeb; you shall strike the rock, waters will exude and the nation shall drink. Moses did so in the presence of the Elders of Israel. (Exodus 17:6)

הִנְנִי עֹמֵד לְפָנֶיךָ שָּׁם עַל־הַצּוּר בְּחֹרֵב וְהִכִּיתָ בַצּוּר וְיָצְאוּ מִמֶּנּוּ מַיִם וְשָׁתָה הָעָם וַיַּעַשׂ כֵּן מֹשֶׁה לְעֵינֵי זִקְנֵי יִשְׂרָאֵל:

It is unnecessary, says the Ramban, for the Torah to repeat the obvious details of this command.

But does the Torah not record God's command as requiring Moses to "speak to the rock"? This phrase, explains the Ramban, should be understood as "speak *about* the rock" – alert the nation that a miracle is about to happen through Moses's hitting the rock!

Alternately, suggests the Ramban, the phrase may be understood as inverted, conveying the directive: *assemble the nation to the rock and speak in their eyes* (in their presence while assembled at the rock). The verse would then be understood as if written as below:

Ramban's Suggested Rephrasing		**Original Torah Text**	
Take the staff	קַח אֶת־הַמַּטֶּה	Take the staff	קַח אֶת־הַמַּטֶּה
and assemble the congregation	וְהַקְהֵל אֶת־הָעֵדָה	and assemble the congregation	וְהַקְהֵל אֶת־הָעֵדָה
to the rock	אֶל־הַסֶּלַע	—	—
you and Aaron your brother	אַתָּה וְאַהֲרֹן אָחִיךָ	you and Aaron your brother	אַתָּה וְאַהֲרֹן אָחִיךָ
speak in their presence	וְדִבַּרְתֶּם לְעֵינֵיהֶם	speak to the rock in their presence	וְדִבַּרְתֶּם אֶל־הַסֶּלַע לְעֵינֵיהֶם
it will give its waters; you will draw out water for them from the rock	וְנָתַן מֵימָיו וְהוֹצֵאתָ לָהֶם מַיִם מִן־הַסָּלַע	it will give its waters; you will draw out water for them from the rock	וְנָתַן מֵימָיו וְהוֹצֵאתָ לָהֶם מַיִם מִן־הַסֶּלַע
and you will provide drink for the congregation and their animals	וְהִשְׁקִיתָ אֶת־הָעֵדָה וְאֶת־בְּעִירָם:	and you will provide drink for the congregation and their animals	וְהִשְׁקִיתָ אֶת־הָעֵדָה וְאֶת־בְּעִירָם:

Even if one were reluctant to accept the rephrasing of God's command, the change from speaking to striking is inconsequential in the Ramban's view. The miracle is just as monumental regardless of whether the rock was spoken to or struck.

The Rambam (Maimonides) sees the transgression not in what Moses did, but in what he said.

Moses and Aaron gathered the congregation in front of the rock and said to them: "Hear, now, you rebellious ones, shall we draw out water for you from this rock?"	וַיַּקְהִלוּ מֹשֶׁה וְאַהֲרֹן אֶת־הַקָּהָל אֶל־פְּנֵי הַסָּלַע וַיֹּאמֶר לָהֶם שִׁמְעוּ־נָא הַמֹּרִים הֲמִן־הַסֶּלַע הַזֶּה נוֹצִיא לָכֶם מָיִם?

"Hear now, you rebellious ones" is an expression of anger unbecoming to Moses and, in the Rambam's opinion, inappropriate to the situation. The Israelites held Moses in the highest possible esteem. When they heard him express himself angrily, they assumed that he was reflecting God's judgment of their actions. Yet, says the Rambam, we do not find that God was upset with the nation's demand for water. Rather, God's immediate response was, "Take the rod, assemble the nation," and so on (20:8), reflecting God's willingness to provide water for the Israelites without criticism. Moses's loss of patience and angry words were not only inappropriate, but also tantamount to a *hillul Hashem* (desecration of the Divine Name).

The Ramban rejects this view as well, noting that nowhere do we find God scolding Moses for being angry. God accuses Moses (and Aaron) of not promoting belief in God and later (20:24) of having defied His command, but not of acting in anger. What about Aaron? God charges him with wrongdoing as well. However, according to the Ramban, Aaron never expressed anger in his life!

These considerations prompt the Ramban to endorse the opinion of Rabbi Hananel, who also sees Moses's sin contained in the verse:

Moses and Aaron gathered the congregation in front of the rock and said to them: "Hear now, you rebellious ones, shall we draw out water for you from this rock?"	וַיַּקְהִלוּ מֹשֶׁה וְאַהֲרֹן אֶת־הַקָּהָל אֶל־פְּנֵי הַסָּלַע וַיֹּאמֶר לָהֶם שִׁמְעוּ־נָא הַמֹּרִים הֲמִן־הַסֶּלַע הַזֶּה נוֹצִיא לָכֶם מָיִם?"

However, for Rabbi Hananel, the key to understanding Moses's misstep may be found in the final segment of the verse:

Shall we draw out water for you from this rock?	הֲמִן־הַסֶּלַע הַזֶּה נוֹצִיא לָכֶם מָיִם?

Moses should have followed the model that he used shortly after the crossing of the sea in response to the nation's complaint of lack of food.

Moses said: When God gives you meat to eat in the evening and bread in the morning [with which] to become sated, when the Lord hears your complaints, which you are complaining against Him, for what are we? Not against us are your complaints, but against the Lord. (Exodus 16:8)	וַיֹּאמֶר מֹשֶׁה, בְּתֵת יְהוָה לָכֶם בָּעֶרֶב בָּשָׂר לֶאֱכֹל וְלֶחֶם בַּבֹּקֶר לִשְׂבֹּעַ בִּשְׁמֹעַ יְהוָה אֶת־תְּלֻנֹּתֵיכֶם אֲשֶׁר־אַתֶּם מַלִּינִם עָלָיו וְנַחְנוּ מָה־ לֹא־עָלֵינוּ תְלֻנֹּתֵיכֶם כִּי עַל־יְהוָה:

Moses and Aaron made it clear at that time that their provisions came from God. He could easily have modified his statement at the rock to name God as the provider. By referring to himself and Aaron as the ones challenged to bring forth water, Moses allowed the nation to attribute the flowing water to himself and to Aaron, not to Divine Intervention. This was the sin. This was the missed opportunity to sanctify God's name.

Nechama Leibowitz, in her weekly study sheet on Parashat Hukat 5729 (1969), promoted the opinion of the *Midrash Devarim Rabbah*, which also cites the phrase "you rebellious ones" as the source of the sin. Yet if we accept the Ramban's critique that those words do not reflect anger, where is the sin? If one suggests that the sin lay in labeling God's nation as "rebellious," how could Moses repeat the same error when he speaks to the nation less than one year later, before its entry to the Land of Israel? There too, Moses says:

Remember, do not forget, that you provoked God your Lord in the desert; from the day you left the Land of Egypt until your arrival at this place, *you have been rebels against God.* (Deuteronomy 9:7)	זְכֹר אַל־תִּשְׁכַּח אֵת אֲשֶׁר־הִקְצַפְתָּ אֶת־יְהוָה אֱלֹהֶיךָ בַּמִּדְבָּר לְמִן־ הַיּוֹם אֲשֶׁר־יָצָאתָ מֵאֶרֶץ מִצְרַיִם עַד־בֹּאֲכֶם עַד־הַמָּקוֹם הַזֶּה מַמְרִים הֱיִיתֶם עִם־יְהוָה:

Nechama Leibowitz offered a solution that reveals the insight of the Midrash and presents a vital message to parents, teachers, employers and all others. Moses's error, according to our sages, was neither in his word choice nor in his tone. Rather, it was in the context in which they were uttered. The nation was not immune to an honest evaluation. But the time when they suffered from thirst was not the appropriate time to rebuke them. Moses should have obeyed God's command to provide water without delay or comment.

Later on, when Moses gathered the nation specifically to provide guidelines for their successful entry into the Land of Israel, it was appropriate for him to refer to them as *mamrim* – rebels. At this later gathering, no immediate threat was facing the people. Their minds were open to reflect on the past with the intention of preparing for the future. But after Miriam's death, when the people faced thirst with no source of water in sight, they had no leisure for reflection or criticism. They needed water. Should they have trusted more in God? Yes. Were they – a nation that received daily sustenance and protection from God – acting in a rebellious manner? Yes. But reproach at that moment was counterproductive. It compromised God's glory and was sinful.

Nechama Leibowitz's insight to the full meaning of *Devarim Rabbah* carries a potent message for those entrusted with the education and rearing of children. Often, children will demand something in an inappropriate manner. When the need is real, the parent or teacher must think quickly: is now the time to criticize or to provide? While I offer no formula here, Nechama's understanding of the Midrash is reminiscent of the guidance offered by Rabbi Shimon ben Elazar:

Do not attempt to appease someone in the moment of his anger. (Avot 4:23)   אַל תְּרַצֶּה אֶת חֲבֵרְךָ בְּשָׁעַת כַּעֲסוֹ.

Sometimes, our preoccupation with our needs makes us unavailable for reflection and growth. In such instances, we can best receive constructive criticism in calmer moments.

.... PUNISHMENT BY GOD

How?

H OW DOES GOD PUNISH? DOES HE SEND AN AGENT TO INFLICT
suffering, or is the sinner deprived of Divine protection and thereby
left vulnerable? A careful reading of an episode in Parashat Hukat
will provide insight into one of the Divine strategies.

After Aaron's death and the Israelites' battle with the Canaanite king
of Arad, the nation continues its journey. But the impending burdens of
travel (and the fact that they had backtracked[1]) prompted them to speak
"against God and against Moses," saying, "Why did you bring us up from
Egypt to die in the wilderness? There is no food and no water, and our soul
is disgusted with the insubstantial food [the manna]" (Numbers 21:5). In
response,

God sent the fiery snakes into the nation and they   וַיְשַׁלַּח יְהוָֹה בָּעָם אֵת הַנְּחָשִׁים
bit the people; a large multitude of Israel died.   הַשְּׂרָפִים וַיְנַשְּׁכוּ אֶת־הָעָם וַיָּמָת
(Numbers 21:6)   עַם־רָב מִיִּשְׂרָאֵל:

To appreciate the Divine action and gain an understanding into God's
ways, we must understand the difference between two similar words, וַיְשַׁלַּח
and וַיִּשְׁלַח. While both may be translated as "he sent," they have distinct
meanings.

From correspondence dated Rosh Hodesh Nisan 5753/March 23, 1993; also based on class,
Beit Midrash L'Torah, 19 Adar I 5733/February 21, 1973.

1 See Rashi on Numbers 21:4.

וַיִּשְׁלַח (va-yishlah) means "he sent on a mission." Examples include:

Jacob sent messengers ahead of him to Esau, his brother to the land of Seir, the field of Edom. (Genesis 32:4)	וַיִּשְׁלַח יַעֲקֹב מַלְאָכִים לְפָנָיו אֶל־עֵשָׂו אָחִיו אַרְצָה שֵׂעִיר שְׂדֵה אֱדוֹם:
Isaac sent Jacob and he went to Padan Aram, to Laban the son of Bethuel the Aramean, brother of Rebecca, mother of Jacob and Esau. (Genesis 28:5) [Isaac sent Jacob on a mission to find a wife.]	וַיִּשְׁלַח יִצְחָק אֶת־יַעֲקֹב וַיֵּלֶךְ פַּדֶּנָה אֲרָם אֶל־לָבָן בֶּן־בְּתוּאֵל הָאֲרַמִּי אֲחִי רִבְקָה אֵם יַעֲקֹב וְעֵשָׂו:
Moses sent them to spy out the Land of Canaan. He said to them, "Ascend here in the south and climb the mountain." (Numbers 13:17)	וַיִּשְׁלַח אֹתָם מֹשֶׁה לָתוּר אֶת־אֶרֶץ כְּנָעַן וַיֹּאמֶר אֲלֵהֶם עֲלוּ זֶה בַּנֶּגֶב וַעֲלִיתֶם אֶת־הָהָר:

One can also send parts of one's body, animals and inanimate objects on a mission. Examples include:

Abraham sent forth his hand and took the knife to slaughter his son. (Genesis 22:10)	וַיִּשְׁלַח אַבְרָהָם אֶת־יָדוֹ וַיִּקַּח אֶת־הַמַּאֲכֶלֶת לִשְׁחֹט אֶת־בְּנוֹ:

וַיְשַׁלַּח (va-yishalah), our second word, means to send off (without giving a mission), let go or release.[2] Examples include:

So it was when God destroyed the cities of the plain that God remembered Abraham. He sent Lot from amidst the upheaval when He overturned the cities in which Lot had lived. (Genesis 19:29)	וַיְהִי בְּשַׁחֵת אֱלֹהִים אֶת־עָרֵי הַכִּכָּר וַיִּזְכֹּר אֱלֹהִים אֶת־אַבְרָהָם וַיְשַׁלַּח אֶת־לוֹט מִתּוֹךְ הַהֲפֵכָה בַּהֲפֹךְ אֶת־הֶעָרִים אֲשֶׁר־יָשַׁב בָּהֵן לוֹט:

---

2 The Shadal on Genesis 3:23 proposes that וַיְשַׁלַּח can be used even when the sender knows the destination to which the person will go. However, it is the person being sent away who decides the destination.

He sent off his brothers and they went. He said to them, "Do not become agitated on the way." (Genesis 45:24)

וַיְשַׁלַּח אֶת־אֶחָיו וַיֵּלֵכוּ וַיֹּאמֶר אֲלֵהֶם אַל־תִּרְגְּזוּ בַּדָּרֶךְ:

Pharaoh gave men orders concerning him and they sent him and his wife and all that was his. (Genesis 12:20) [In this verse, וַיְשַׁלְּחוּ (*va-yishalhu*) can also mean "they escorted." See Ibn Ezra he-Aroch and Hizkuni.]

וַיְצַו עָלָיו פַּרְעֹה אֲנָשִׁים וַיְשַׁלְּחוּ אֹתוֹ וְאֶת־אִשְׁתּוֹ וְאֶת־כָּל־אֲשֶׁר־לוֹ:

The Lord said to Moses, "Come to Pharaoh and tell him, 'Thus said the Lord: Send out [*shalah*] My people that they may serve Me.'" (Exodus 7:26)

וַיֹּאמֶר יְהוָֹה אֶל־מֹשֶׁה בֹּא אֶל־פַּרְעֹה וְאָמַרְתָּ אֵלָיו כֹּה אָמַר יְהוָֹה שַׁלַּח אֶת־עַמִּי וְיַעַבְדֻנִי:

When the word שַׁלַּח / וַיְשַׁלַּח is used, it makes no difference if the one being sent wants to leave or not. We are commanded:

You shall surely send away the mother and take the young for yourself, so that it will be good for you and you will prolong your days. (Deuteronomy 22:7)

שַׁלֵּחַ תְּשַׁלַּח אֶת־הָאֵם וְאֶת־הַבָּנִים תִּקַּח־לָךְ לְמַעַן יִיטַב לָךְ וְהַאֲרַכְתָּ יָמִים:

The mother bird must be sent away regardless if she wishes to leave her young or not. Similarly, a Jewish slave (*eved Ivri*), in the normative instance, is to be sent out after six years whether he wishes to leave or not.[3] As the Torah states:

If your brother, a Hebrew man or a Hebrew woman, is sold to you, he shall serve you for six years, and in the seventh year you shall send him away from you free. (Deuteronomy 15:12)

כִּי־יִמָּכֵר לְךָ אָחִיךָ הָעִבְרִי אוֹ הָעִבְרִיָּה וַעֲבָדְךָ שֵׁשׁ שָׁנִים וּבַשָּׁנָה הַשְּׁבִיעִת תְּשַׁלְּחֶנּוּ חָפְשִׁי מֵעִמָּךְ:

Now let us ask: Were the snakes, which were referred to in the beginning of this chapter, sent directly as messengers of God or merely released? Were

---

3 While the Torah allows the insistent Jewish slave to remain with his master after his six years of service, the compromised status is marked by the piercing of the Jewish slave's ear.

they imported for this specific purpose or indigenous to the area? Should the language of the verse describing the Divine act employ the word וַיְשַׁלַּח (va-yishlah) or וַיְשַׁלַּח (va-yishalah)?

One would likely propose that the word should be וַיְשַׁלַּח (va-yishlah), suggesting that the snakes were sent to the scene as agents of God specifically to punish the Israelites. However, the Torah actually uses the word וַיְשַׁלַּח (va-yishalah), implying that God did not import the snakes or command them to bite. Rather, He merely released them. But, we must ask, from where?

Early in Deuteronomy (8:15), the Torah describes the desert as "great and awesome," filled with "snake, fiery serpent and scorpion." Nechama Leibowitz explained that the snakes were always present and that it was their nature to bite. However, God restrained the snakes from their tendency to injure as one of the many ways in which He protected the Israelites. When the Israelites sinned, God ended this aspect of His protection and let the snakes do as they wished. While the snakes served as the vehicle through which punishment was inflicted, they were not directly sent as messengers with a command to injure. The snakes were merely allowed to act as snakes act.[4] While those who merited Divine protection may have been spared their bite, those who sinned were subject to the natural forces already present in their environment.[5]

In this episode, punishment was delivered by removing an aspect of *hashgaha pratit*, Divine Providence, and subjecting human beings to natural elements. At times, God delivers retribution through other means. God's world contains many potential hazards. Through Divine mercy and grace, we are spared from harm, for which we thank God in our daily Amidah prayer.[6]

---

4 As a support to the thesis presented, Nechama Leibowitz noted that the definite article ("the") is used in the biblical verse (Numbers 21:6) referring to "the fiery snakes," and not merely "fiery snakes." Thus, grammatically, the Torah is referring to snakes of which we have already been told; *the* snakes are the same as the snakes that are identified in Deuteronomy (8:15): "Who leads you through the great and awesome wilderness of snake, fiery serpent and scorpion, and thirst where there was no water, Who brings forth water for you from the rock of flint."

5 Author's elaboration.

6 Author's comment.

TWO SONS AND A MESSAGE
FOR GENERATIONS

MAY JEWS QUESTION? DOES OUR TRADITIONAL NEGATIVE view of the Wicked Son from the Haggadah guide us to avoid asking questions? Definitely not! A careful review of the verse that contains the Wicked Son's question reveals that he never actually asks a question.

In presenting the curiosity of the Wise Son, the Torah states:

When your child asks you tomorrow, saying, "What are the testimonies, statutes and laws which God our Lord has commanded you?" (Deuteronomy 6:20)

כִּי־יִשְׁאָלְךָ בִנְךָ מָחָר לֵאמֹר מָה הָעֵדֹת וְהַחֻקִּים וְהַמִּשְׁפָּטִים אֲשֶׁר צִוָּה יְהוָה אֱלֹהֵינוּ אֶתְכֶם:

Notice, though, that the Wicked Son does not actually ask a question.

When your children shall **say** to you, "What is [the purpose of] this service to you?" (Exodus 12:26)

וְהָיָה כִּי־יֹאמְרוּ אֲלֵיכֶם בְּנֵיכֶם מָה הָעֲבֹדָה הַזֹּאת לָכֶם:

This person, whom the Haggadah defines as wicked, is making a statement. He has no question to ask and is not interested in an answer. While it is always good and even desirable to have a genuine question, a rhetorical attack distances a person from his people.

From conversation with Nechama Leibowitz on 5 Nisan 5752/April 8, 1992.

The Torah's verses conceal a message of hope. When the Torah introduces the Wise Son's question, it uses the word מָחָר, tomorrow, which refers to all future generations. This qualification does not appear regarding the Wicked Son. Its absence imparts the message that the day may come when no children will ever again wish to attack the Torah's value system.

A CONTRAST OF RESPONSIBILITIES

H OW DOES THE OBLIGATION OF A CITIZEN IN A TORAH SOCI-
ety differ from that in a secular state? Nechama shared with me an
observation related to her by the Israeli jurist and former deputy
attorney general, Professor Nachum Rackover. The comment is based on
the verses below which establish the mitzvah of *hashavat aveda*, returning
lost articles.

You shall not see the ox of your brother or his sheep going astray and hide yourself from them; you shall (surely) return them to your brother. If your brother is not near to you or you do not know him, you shall gather it into your house and it shall be with you until your brother demands it and you return it to him. So shall you do for his donkey, so shall you do for his garment, so shall you do for every lost article of your brother that will become lost from him and you find it; you may not hide yourself. (Deuteronomy 22:1-8)	לֹא־תִרְאֶה אֶת־שׁוֹר אָחִיךָ אוֹ אֶת־שֵׂיוֹ נִדָּחִים וְהִתְעַלַּמְתָּ מֵהֶם הָשֵׁב תְּשִׁיבֵם לְאָחִיךָ: וְאִם־לֹא קָרוֹב אָחִיךָ אֵלֶיךָ וְלֹא יְדַעְתּוֹ וַאֲסַפְתּוֹ אֶל־תּוֹךְ בֵּיתֶךָ וְהָיָה עִמְּךָ עַד דְּרֹשׁ אָחִיךָ אֹתוֹ וַהֲשֵׁבֹתוֹ לוֹ: וְכֵן תַּעֲשֶׂה לַחֲמֹרוֹ וְכֵן תַּעֲשֶׂה לְשִׂמְלָתוֹ וְכֵן תַּעֲשֶׂה לְכָל־ אֲבֵדַת אָחִיךָ אֲשֶׁר־תֹּאבַד מִמֶּנּוּ וּמְצָאתָהּ לֹא תוּכַל לְהִתְעַלֵּם:

Professor Rackover noted that in secular civil law, we are not obligated to
retrieve the lost property of others even if it lies directly before us. If we

From conversation with Nechama Leibowitz during a visit on 13 Elul 5753/August 29,
1993.

choose to take hold of the item, then we are required by law to submit it to the appropriate local authority. Otherwise, we are not obligated to be concerned about this property or to be worried for the concern of the one who lost it. In Torah law, by contrast, if one encounters lost property that its owner can identify, one is (usually[1]) obligated to occupy himself with the protection and return of the article.

In secular civil law, a government cannot obligate its residents to perform beneficial acts or to be concerned for others. A government can only require that one not harm others. In fact, in a democratic society there are only two obligations that require action: the payment of taxes and service in the armed forces. All other obligations require abstinence from wrongdoing. The Torah obligates us to concern ourselves with the welfare of others.

In a separate conversation, Nechama Leibowitz, speaking to me in my role as a pulpit rabbi at the time, expressed her concern about helping those Jews who were not fully committed to discover the beauty of the Torah. She advanced the position that it is helpful to enable individuals to understand the difference between the laws of general society, with which they are familiar, and the Torah's apparently similar yet quite different laws. Nechama thought that knowledge of Jewish law would lead to a deeper appreciation of the Torah's approach to life. The return of lost property is a clear example of the Torah's higher expectations.

In reviewing the verses cited above, one may identify several questions. One of the questions that Rashi addresses is why it is necessary to include the phrase

until your brother demands it.   עַד דְּרֹשׁ אָחִיךָ אֹתוֹ

---

1 Nechama Leibowitz noted that the syntax of the opening verse that we are currently studying is unusual: לֹא־תִרְאֶה . . . וְהִתְעַלַּמְתָּ (You shall not see . . . and hide yourself).

This use of words is found only here in verse 1 and again in verse 4. The normal biblical style would be כִּי תִרְאֶה . . . לֹא תוּכַל לְהִתְעַלֵּם (When you see . . . you may not hide yourself).

The unusual phrasing, which moves the negative to the beginning of verse 1 and allows the verb "hide" to stand independently, is the basis for a classical teaching. There may be times when the Torah permits one to hide or ignore a lost article. Such cases include instances when the object's retrieval would compromise the finder's dignity or require more financial outlay than the item's value.

Would we think, asks Rashi, that he will return the found item before the owner asked for it? (This is impossible, as the owner is not yet known to the finder!) Rashi answers:

demand of him [i.e., investigate him] to verify that   דְּרְשֵׁהוּ שֶׁלֹּא יְהֵא רַמָּאי
he is not a deceiver.

The Siftei Hachamim, a commentary on Rashi, explains that according to Rashi's understanding of the verse, the word אֹתוֹ, "it," which can also mean "him," refers to אָחִיךָ, your brother. The phrase should be read: investigate him, your brother, to ascertain he is the true owner and not a deceiver.

Nechama added that Rashi's explanation is also constructed on the basis of a second meaning carried by the word אֹתוֹ, "it/him." The word אֹתוֹ can also be understood as הָאוֹת שֶׁלּוֹ, his sign. The Baal ha-Turim adopts this approach in his commentary. He understands the phrase as instructing the finder to investigate the unique sign given by the one claiming the object to ascertain that he is honest and not a deceiver.

Despite Nechama's understanding of Rashi's comment, she described the comment as "strange." She saw it as deviating from the plain meaning of the text. Yet Nechama was at a loss to offer an alternative answer to Rashi's question. Although she had searched many commentaries on Rashi, she could not find any other solution.

A MATTER OF PERSPECTIVE

HE BIBLE RECORDS SEVERAL EPISODES IN WHICH ANGELS communicate with people. At times, the people involved realize what is happening, but in other instances, they do not. One of these experiences provides insight into both the behavior of angels and the functioning of human perception. Simultaneously, the episode illustrates how subtleties in introductory phrases can reveal a story within a story.

Samson's birth is foretold to his mother, who has been childless until now. She is told that her child is to be a Nazarite even while in the womb. Therefore, she may not drink wine or any other alcoholic beverages, and must abstain from eating ritually impure food during her pregnancy. Uncertain about the nature of the being she has encountered, she shares her experience with Manoah, her husband.

The Book of Judges relates:

The woman came and said to her husband, saying, "A man of God came to me, and his appearance was like the appearance of an angel of God, very awesome, and I did not ask him from where he was and his name he did not tell me." (Judges 13:6)	וַתָּבֹא הָאִשָּׁה וַתֹּאמֶר לְאִישָׁהּ לֵאמֹר אִישׁ הָאֱלֹהִים בָּא אֵלַי וּמַרְאֵהוּ כְּמַרְאֵה מַלְאַךְ הָאֱלֹהִים נוֹרָא מְאֹד וְלֹא שְׁאִלְתִּיהוּ אֵי־מִזֶּה הוּא וְאֶת־שְׁמוֹ לֹא־הִגִּיד לִי:

Who was the messenger?

From conversation with Nechama Leibowitz during a visit on 23 Tammuz 5753/August 9, 1993.

Manoah's wife allows for the possibility that he was a prophet (a "man of God") or, because of his awe-inspiring appearance, perhaps even an angel. What is Manoah's impression of the messenger?

After listening to his wife's account of the encounter, Manoah prays to God, asking Him to send the "man of God" once more to provide instruction for the proper care of the child. The text tells us:

9. God hearkened to the voice of Manoah; the angel of God came again to the woman and she was sitting in the field and Manoah, her husband, was not with her.

(ט) וַיִּשְׁמַע הָאֱ־לֹהִים בְּקוֹל מָנוֹחַ וַיָּבֹא מַלְאַךְ הָאֱ־לֹהִים עוֹד אֶל־הָאִשָּׁה וְהִיא יוֹשֶׁבֶת בַּשָּׂדֶה וּמָנוֹחַ אִישָׁהּ אֵין עִמָּהּ:

10. The woman hurried, ran and told to her husband; she said to him, "Behold, there has appeared to me the man who came to me on that day."

(י) וַתְּמַהֵר הָאִשָּׁה וַתָּרָץ וַתַּגֵּד לְאִישָׁהּ וַתֹּאמֶר אֵלָיו הִנֵּה נִרְאָה אֵלַי הָאִישׁ אֲשֶׁר־בָּא בַיּוֹם אֵלָי:

11. Manoah arose and went after his wife; he came to the man and said to him, "Are you the man that spoke to the woman?" He said, "I am." (Judges 13:9-11)

(יא) וַיָּקָם וַיֵּלֶךְ מָנוֹחַ אַחֲרֵי אִשְׁתּוֹ וַיָּבֹא אֶל־הָאִישׁ וַיֹּאמֶר לוֹ הַאַתָּה הָאִישׁ אֲשֶׁר־דִּבַּרְתָּ אֶל־הָאִשָּׁה וַיֹּאמֶר אָנִי:

Despite the fact that verse 9 specifies that God sent "the angel of God," Manoah sees him only as "the man," perhaps not even a prophet (which would be conveyed by the description "man of God"). When does Manoah realize that he and his wife were privileged to communicate with an angel of God?

In the chapter entitled "The Bud Vase and Use of Proper Names in the Biblical Text," we established that the Torah is parsimonious in its use of words. When the identity of a character is apparent from the text, the Torah will usually not name him when he speaks. This is especially true when the speaker has already been identified in a previous verse within the given episode. But look at the verses below and their references to the angel.

12. Manoah said, "Now your words will come forth, what shall be the rule for the lad and his doing?"

(יב) וַיֹּאמֶר מָנוֹחַ עַתָּה יָבֹא דְבָרֶיךָ מַה־יִּהְיֶה מִשְׁפַּט־הַנַּעַר וּמַעֲשֵׂהוּ:

13. The angel of the Lord said to Manoah, "Of all

(יג) וַיֹּאמֶר מַלְאַךְ יְהֹוָה אֶל־מָנוֹחַ

that I said to the woman shall she beware.

מִכֹּל אֲשֶׁר־אָמַרְתִּי אֶל־הָאִשָּׁה תִּשָּׁמֵר:

14. From all that comes out of the grapevine she shall not eat, and wine or strong drink she may not drink, and any unclean [thing] she may not eat; all that I commanded her shall she observe."

(יד) מִכֹּל אֲשֶׁר־יֵצֵא מִגֶּפֶן הַיַּיִן לֹא תֹאכַל וְיַיִן וְשֵׁכָר אַל־תֵּשְׁתְּ וְכָל־טֻמְאָה אַל־תֹּאכַל כֹּל אֲשֶׁר־צִוִּיתִיהָ תִּשְׁמֹר:

15. Manoah said to the angel of the Lord, "Let us take you in now and prepare for you a young goat."

(טו) וַיֹּאמֶר מָנוֹחַ אֶל־מַלְאַךְ יְהֹוָה נַעְצְרָה־נָּא אוֹתָךְ וְנַעֲשֶׂה לְפָנֶיךָ גְּדִי עִזִּים:

16. The angel of the Lord said to Manoah, "If you take me in, I will not eat of your bread, but if you are going to offer a burnt-offering, offer it to the Lord," for Manoah did not know that he was an angel of the Lord. (Judges 13:12-16)

(טז) וַיֹּאמֶר מַלְאַךְ יְהֹוָה אֶל־מָנוֹחַ אִם־תַּעְצְרֵנִי לֹא־אֹכַל בְּלַחְמֶךָ וְאִם־תַּעֲשֶׂה עֹלָה לַיהֹוָה תַּעֲלֶנָּה כִּי לֹא־יָדַע מָנוֹחַ כִּי־מַלְאַךְ יְהֹוָה הוּא:

Why in verse 13 and again in verse 16 are we told, "The angel of the Lord said to Manoah"? It should suffice to say "He said" or at the most "He said to Manoah." The wordy introductory phrase, "The angel of the Lord said to Manoah" alerts the reader to a strategy that the angel is employing. He never declares his true essence. Yet the elaborate identification ("The angel of the Lord") reflects his attempt to convey his true identity through non-verbal communication. Each statement was deliberately delivered in a fashion that would help Manoah discover the angel's identity.

Was the angel successful? When does Manoah catch on and realize that he is in the presence of an angel? Verse 16 informs us that Manoah offered him food because "Manoah did not know that he was an angel of the Lord." And yet, in the previous verse, the text states, "Manoah said to the angel of the Lord." How can the text state that Manoah addressed his remarks to an angel when he was still unaware of the angel's true identity? In fact, it is not until he sees the messenger ascend with the offering (verses 20–21) that both Manoah and his wife fall to the ground on their faces in awe. As the text tells us:

17. Manoah said to the angel of the Lord, "What is your name, that when your word comes true we may do you honor?"

(יז) וַיֹּאמֶר מָנוֹחַ אֶל־מַלְאַךְ יְהֹוָה מִי שְׁמֶךָ כִּי־יָבֹא דְבָרְךָ וְכִבַּדְנוּךָ:

18. The angel of the Lord said to him, "Why do you ask for my name? It is hidden."

(יח) וַיֹּאמֶר לוֹ מַלְאַךְ יְהוָה לָמָּה זֶּה תִּשְׁאַל לִשְׁמִי וְהוּא־פֶלִאי:

19. Manoah took the kid goat and the meal-offering and offered it upon the rock to the Lord; he [the angel] performed a miracle as Manoah and his wife looked on.

(יט) וַיִּקַּח מָנוֹחַ אֶת־גְּדִי הָעִזִּים וְאֶת־הַמִּנְחָה וַיַּעַל עַל־הַצּוּר לַיהוָה וּמַפְלִא לַעֲשׂוֹת וּמָנוֹחַ וְאִשְׁתּוֹ רֹאִים:

20. And it was as the flame went up from upon the altar toward heaven, the angel of the Lord ascended in the flame of the altar; Manoah and his wife looked on and they fell on their faces to the ground.

(כ) וַיְהִי בַעֲלוֹת הַלַּהַב מֵעַל הַמִּזְבֵּחַ הַשָּׁמַיְמָה וַיַּעַל מַלְאַךְ־יְהוָה בְּלַהַב הַמִּזְבֵּחַ וּמָנוֹחַ וְאִשְׁתּוֹ רֹאִים וַיִּפְּלוּ עַל־פְּנֵיהֶם אָרְצָה:

21. . . . then Manoah knew that he was an angel of the Lord.[1] (Judges 13:17–21)

(כא) וְלֹא־יָסַף עוֹד מַלְאַךְ יְהוָה לְהֵרָאֹה אֶל־מָנוֹחַ וְאֶל־אִשְׁתּוֹ אָז יָדַע מָנוֹחַ כִּי־מַלְאַךְ יְהוָה הוּא:

Our question – how can the text state, "Manoah said to the angel of the Lord" if Manoah has yet to acknowledge him as an angel? – is valid only if we assume that the text's identification of a situation, or in our case a character, reflects the speaker's (i.e. Manoah's) view of life and not the objective one of the "narrator." In our case, when verse 15 states, "Manoah said to the angel of the Lord," is the text revealing Manoah's perception or that of the omniscient narrator?

I suggested to Nechama Leibowitz that once a verb is recorded indicating an action that is to be performed by the identified (or understood character), then the full introductory phrase reflects that character's perspective. In our story, then, the text reveals to us that Manoah begins to sense that he is in the presence of an angel before he is rationally prepared to reach the same conclusion. His intuitive faculty has been receptive to the angel's clues. Therefore, the text introduces Manoah's remarks in both verses 15 and 17, stating, "Manoah said to the angel of the Lord," but Manoah's rational faculty is not yet convinced.

Nechama Leibowitz endorsed my conclusions and thanked me for

---

1 According to commentators, the first part of verse 21 is a parenthetical statement; the last phrase, quoted above, is the direct continuation of the flow of the story.

revealing the subtleties in the chapter. However, Nechama shared with me that she was uncertain as to whether there were a uniform rule that could be applied throughout the Bible.

Sometime after Nechama's death, I identified a proof to support my conclusions in the context of Manoah's encounter with the angel of God.

If we were to attribute the text's statement in verse 15, "Manoah said to the angel of the Lord" as the "narrator's" comment rather than as an insight to Manoah's thinking, we should expect this perspective to hold true throughout the episode. Yet in verse 11. the narrative text states, "He came to the man and said to him." If the text were to be speaking from the objective perspective of the narrator, it should have said: He came to the angel of God and said to him. This lack of parallelism supports the observation that the introductory phrases used in our chapter reflect the perspectives of the characters named within it.

With this understanding, the chapter describing the announcement of the forthcoming conception of Samson teaches insights about both angels and humans. A Divine celestial emissary may choose (or be commanded) not to reveal his identity overtly. The human encountering such an angel is challenged to perceive the full scope of his experience. The episode also reveals to us that our spiritual and intuitive faculties have the potential to discover layers of reality that our rational minds do not perceive as easily.

MORE ON PERSPECTIVE AND NAMES

Rebecca's Follow-Up Directive to Jacob

A S ISAAC AGED AND REFLECTED ON THE POSSIBILITY THAT THE end of his life was approaching, he summoned his firstborn son, Esau. He asked Esau to go out to the field, hunt game and prepare him a meal, after which he would bless him. Since Isaac ended his command with the words בְּטֶרֶם אָמוּת, before I die, Rebecca concludes that the blessing to which her husband was referring was important – and she felt that Esau was not the one who should receive it.

With Isaac nearly blind and Esau off hunting deer, Rebecca encourages Jacob to disguise himself as his older brother, serve a meal which Rebecca will cook immediately and secure the blessing for himself. Jacob carries out the plan and receives blessings from his father. When Esau realizes that he has been tricked, he is hurt and angry. He resolves that once Isaac dies, he will murder Jacob in revenge.

Rebecca, informed of Esau's resolution, now faces a painful decision: how will she protect one son from the other? As the Torah relates the new developments, Rebecca's level of understanding of the complexity of her sons' relationship is now revealed.

The Torah tells us:

Rebecca was told of the words of Esau, her older son. She sent for and summoned Jacob, her younger son, and she said to him, "Behold, Esau, your	וַיֻּגַּד לְרִבְקָה אֶת־דִּבְרֵי עֵשָׂו בְּנָהּ הַגָּדֹל וַתִּשְׁלַח וַתִּקְרָא לְיַעֲקֹב בְּנָהּ הַקָּטָן וַתֹּאמֶר אֵלָיו הִנֵּה עֵשָׂו

From conversation with Nechama Leibowitz on 24 Kislev 5756/December 17, 1995.

brother, is consoling himself by planning to kill you. So now, my son, heed my voice and arise, flee to Laban, my brother, to Haran. Dwell with him a short while until your brother's wrath subsides." (Genesis 27:42–44)

אָחִיךָ מִתְנַחֵם לְךָ לְהָרְגֶךָ: וְעַתָּה בְנִי שְׁמַע בְּקֹלִי וְקוּם בְּרַח־לְךָ אֶל־לָבָן אָחִי חָרָנָה: וְיָשַׁבְתָּ עִמּוֹ יָמִים אֲחָדִים עַד אֲשֶׁר־תָּשׁוּב חֲמַת אָחִיךָ:

As we read these three verses, we must ask ourselves: why are there apparently redundant references to our characters? Why, when Rebecca is informed of Esau's intentions, does the Torah text identify him as Esau, her older son? Similarly, why the double description when the text tells us that Rebecca sent for Jacob, her younger son? In fact, it should have been possible to reduce the verbiage of the verse even further by eliminating the reference to Esau. The Torah could have said: Rebecca was told of the words of her son. She sent for and summoned Jacob, and told him . . . .

To appreciate the depth of meaning concealed in these references, we must ask ourselves another question: whose perspective is conveyed in the opening phrase of the verses cited above ("Rebecca was told of the words of Esau, her older son")? There are two possibilities: it is either Rebecca's or that of God, who is narrating the text. Nechama Leibowitz believed that the Torah was speaking from Rebecca's perspective. As such, she said, we are given the insight that Rebecca "knew very well that he [Esau] was the older one" and was entitled to Isaac's blessing.

When the Torah adds Esau's proper name in addition to his position as the firstborn, we are taught that Rebecca further understands that her son, through the part of his personality reflected by his name Esau (an אִישׁ יֹדֵעַ צַיִד, one who knows hunting[1]), is capable of harming Jacob.[2] Nechama said, "She must tell Jacob (who, as an אִישׁ תָּם, a wholesome man who spends his time in the tents of study,[3] will not know how to repel an attack by Esau[4]) that he must flee." According to this reading of the text, Rebecca has

---

1 See Genesis 25:27.

2 This observation was suggested by the author and accepted by Professor Leibowitz.

3 See Genesis 25:27.

4 Author's comment.

achieved a thorough understanding of the dynamics of this confrontation on her own.[5]

However, Nechama said that it is not possible to know with certainty that the opening phrase is written from Rebecca's perspective. It may be that the text is written to reflect the perspective of the source of the information shared with Rebecca, which, according to our sages in *Midrash Rabbah*, was Divine inspiration.[6] As such, the source, an objective one, is informing Rebecca that by engineering a plan that deprived her older son of a blessing presumed to belong to the firstborn, she created a volatile situation. Rebecca is told further that as Esau (not just "son" or "firstborn"), her son is capable of harming Jacob. Rebecca accepts God's message, as

---

5 A possible support to the position that the phrase *Rebecca was told of the words of Esau, her older son*, is spoken from Rebecca's perspective may be garnered from a careful reading of the verses describing Rebecca's actions following her hearing Isaac's command to Esau.

וְרִבְקָה אָמְרָה אֶל־יַעֲקֹב בְּנָהּ לֵאמֹר הִנֵּה שָׁמַעְתִּי אֶת־אָבִיךָ מְדַבֵּר אֶל־עֵשָׂו אָחִיךָ לֵאמֹר:

Rebecca said to Jacob, her son, "Behold, I heard your father speaking to Esau, your brother, saying . . ." (Genesis 27:6).

Rebecca appears to ignore the birth order. She views Jacob as *her son*; not as her younger son. This is consistent with her decision to make sure that Jacob received the blessing that Isaac had intended for Esau. However, as events proceed, we are told:

וַתִּקַּח רִבְקָה אֶת־בִּגְדֵי עֵשָׂו בְּנָהּ הַגָּדֹל הַחֲמֻדֹת אֲשֶׁר אִתָּהּ בַּבָּיִת וַתַּלְבֵּשׁ אֶת־יַעֲקֹב בְּנָהּ הַקָּטָן:

Rebecca took the special garments of Esau, her older son, that were with her in the house, and dressed Jacob, her younger son. (Genesis 27:15)

Though at first Rebecca ignored Esau's status as the firstborn son, she later reflects on the potential conflict that she is creating. The reality is that Esau is the firstborn. It is he – and not Jacob, the younger son – whom Isaac wishes to bless at that moment.

Alternatively, one could advance the position that here, too, the narrator's perspective is presented. I believe it is more difficult to support this position.

6 The Torah tells us:

וַיִּשְׂטֹם עֵשָׂו אֶת־יַעֲקֹב עַל־הַבְּרָכָה אֲשֶׁר בֵּרֲכוֹ אָבִיו וַיֹּאמֶר עֵשָׂו בְּלִבּוֹ יִקְרְבוּ יְמֵי אֵבֶל אָבִי וְאַהַרְגָה אֶת־יַעֲקֹב אָחִי:

Esau despised Jacob because of the blessing with which his father had blessed him. He said in his heart [i.e., to himself]: "Let the days of my father's mourning approach, and I will kill Jacob, my brother" (Genesis 27:41).

As Esau's resolution was a mental one, only God could know of his intention.

reflected in the text that describes Rebecca's summoning of Jacob, "her younger son."[7]

Whether the phrase, "Rebecca was told of the words of Esau, her older son," reflects Rebecca's realization of the difficult situation now confronting Jacob or conveys the message of God to her, Rebecca understands clearly that she must now prevail upon her younger son to flee from the wrath of his powerful brother.

In speaking directly to Jacob, Rebecca uses a double reference:

Behold, Esau your brother is consoling himself by planning to kill you.   הִנֵּה עֵשָׂו אָחִיךָ מִתְנַחֵם לְךָ לְהָרְגֶךָ

Yet as Rebecca continues to outline her plan, she tells Jacob that he should stay with Laban until

until your brother's wrath subsides.   אֲשֶׁר־תָּשׁוּב חֲמַת אָחִיךָ

Note that Rebecca no longer uses the double reference to Esau. She identifies him only as "your brother." Perhaps this reflects a resolution of the current conflict between Esau and Jacob as Rebecca envisions it: eventually her older son will interact with Jacob only as his brother, dismissing from his mind the physical harm that Esau is capable of inflicting.[8]

In conveying the details of her plan, Rebecca tells Jacob:

Now, my son, heed my voice.   וְעַתָּה בְנִי שְׁמַע בְּקֹלִי

Why did Rebecca add that which was obvious – "my son?" Nechama suggested that Rebecca was not just offering good advice. Rather, Rebecca

---

7 Author's comment. Based on Nechama's general position that there is no definite rule for determining perspective, it is possible that both descriptive phrases reflect the narrator's perspective. If so, the phrase describing Esau may be intended to teach Rebecca that she should have anticipated negative consequences for her act of deception. The phrase identifying Jacob as her younger son may be directed to the reader, emphasizing the confrontation's source.

8 Author's comment.

was telling Jacob, "I am speaking as your mother, and I command you. This is a matter of respecting parents." Rebecca expected Jacob to take the necessary precautionary steps to protect his life. Alternatively, it may be a reflection of Rebecca's deep love for Jacob.[9]

---

9 While this observation was suggested by the author and accepted by Professor Leibowitz as a possible understanding of the text, I believe that Nechama's understanding is more accurate. Note that in directing Jacob to the steps he should take in appearing before his father, Rebecca says,

וְעַתָּה בְנִי שְׁמַע בְּקֹלִי לַאֲשֶׁר אֲנִי מְצַוָּה אֹתָךְ:

Listen, now my son, to my voice, to that which I command you. (Genesis 27:8)

Here, Rebecca orders Jacob explicitly to take action. When the first part of this verse ("Listen now, my son") is used later in the story, it is likely meant to be, as Nechama proposed, a command to action.

I ASK QUESTIONS

N THE SUMMER OF 5753 (1993), MY FAMILY TRAVELED TO ISRAEL to celebrate my son, Ari, becoming a *bar mitzvah*. I was eager to have Nechama Leibowitz join us for the simha (joyous occassion). Before I departed for Israel, Nechama had already told me that she was elderly and it was very difficult for her to leave her apartment.

Having arrived in Israel, I extended an invitation once again, including an offer to have a car service transport her to and from our celebration. She politely declined. Although I was disappointed, I understood her circumstances. I asked her whether she would allow me to videotape a message from her to Ari. I expected an immediate rejection to this idea, as Nechama never approved the taping of her classes.[1] While she declined this invitation

---

From conversations with Nechama Leibowitz during visits on 5 Elul 5753/August 21, 1993 and 13 Elul 5753/August 29, 1993.

1 At the Conference for the Advancement of Jewish Education (CAJE) in 1988 at The Hebrew University, Nechama entered a lecture hall overflowing with Jewish educators eager to learn from and with her. She was flabbergasted by the size of the audience; but as she approached the podium, she insisted that all recording devices be turned off.

During my visits in Elul 5753 (August 1993), I broached the topic of recording her lectures. I told Nechama that I was listening to tapes of Rabbi Josef Soloveitchik and was able to learn from him even then. (The Rav was already deceased at the time.) Nechama, who had listened to some of the Rav's tapes and enjoyed them (she said that the one on Parashat Be-ha'alotcha was fabulous), said, "If I had things to say like Rav Soloveitchik, I would also allow recording." I followed her as she moved into the kitchen. Nechama then added, "I don't speak from a text. Sometimes I tell a joke in the middle. Does my joke need to be preserved for generations? Sometimes I may say nonsense."

as well, her response, which was other than the one I anticipated, provides insight to her approach to teaching Torah.

"I am not a *darshanit*," she said. "It is not my method to give speeches, but to ask questions. Not even once have I lectured."

Nechama Leibowitz was a zealous proponent of the use of questioning in teaching. Questions, which facilitate active learning for all participants, often empower learners to discover answers rather than being told the answers. (In Nechama's classes, whether they were small groups in yeshivot and seminaries or large classes at universities, Nechama required each student to write an answer to her questions. She would rotate or call students to her desk to check each answer!)

Nechama enjoyed teaching a variety of students. Once she gave a class to women in an Israeli *moshav* community in the vicinity of Kiryat Gat. The participants were unskilled laborers, cleaning personnel, Egged ticket clerks, and so on. As the class was held on Rosh Hodesh,[2] Nechama chose Psalm 104, *Barchi nafshi*, as the subject. She asked the women to identify one verse that could serve as a title for the chapter. One participant responded, "Here we have to think!" Another said, "We need time." "I'm giving you time," Nechama answered. "I'm not running away."

With that encouragement, each student placed her finger on the appropriate verse. (From Nechama's account of the story, it appears that placing the finger was an alternative to writing an answer.) Nechama then asked them, "Why does the psalm begin with a reference to light?" "Because the Torah begins with light," they answered.

As the class progressed, one of the women, prompted by Nechama's question, observed, "God is depicted as very great and human beings as very small." "*Yafeh me'od* (very nice)," Nechama remarked. Excitedly, the woman turned to her friend, saying, "She said that I answered well!"

For one hour and fifteen minutes these women, who were not deeply involved in Torah study, sat and learned together with a biblical scholar. Nechama reflected, "I thought to myself – this is the nation of Israel! I did not know people like these and on this evening I got to know them. They

---

2 Rosh Hodesh is the beginning of a new month in the Jewish calendar. At the conclusion of the morning prayer service, Psalm 104 is added.

are pleasant. These young women are so very nice. If you give them time to think, they know the answers."

Among the foundations of Nechama's methodology are the following principles:

• Challenge the learners to think.
• Give them time to discover.
• Guide them with the presentation of a question.

Through these principles, Nechama Leibowitz empowered countless people to enjoy learning Torah and to be effective teachers of Torah.[3]

---

3 I am proud to consider myself a student of both the learning and the methodology of Professor Nechama Leibowitz. The following episode reveals the influence of Nechama's *derech* (method) on my own teaching.

During my summer vacation, my family and I would frequently visit my in-laws, who lived in southern New Jersey for five decades. On Shabbat, we attended a private synagogue hosted by Mr. Jack Trocki, a philanthropist who did all he could to support a vibrant Jewish community. Mr. Trocki would invite visiting rabbis, scholars and community leaders to conduct Shabbat afternoon classes. I was a frequent volunteer.

One Shabbat, Daniel Kurzer, the former United States ambassador to Israel and at the time a staff member of the US State Department, was visiting. Mr. Kurzer was also a frequent speaker at Mr. Trocki's synagogue. That Shabbat, when Mr. Trocki invited me to lead an afternoon class, I demurred, explaining that I looked forward to hearing Daniel Kurzer. I believe we both spoke that week. When Mr. Trocki introduced me, he mentioned that I had been hesitant to speak at first. He did not understand why, since "all Rabbi Yasgur does is ask us questions and we do all the work!"

B"H 18 Tammuz

My dear friends

[I extend] blessings of Mazal Tov on your happy occasion.
Regrettably, my current health condition does not allow
me an excursion like this from my home, and therefore I
will not be able to join in your celebration.
But, my good blessings to you that your son should grow
in Torah, in wisdom and in reverence for God.
I extend to you peaceful tidings,

Nechama L.

ב"ה יח' בתמוז
ידידי הטובים
ברכות מזל טוב ליום שמחתכם
לצערי מצב בריאותי היום אינו מאפשר
לי יציאה כזו מביתי ולכן לא אוכל להשתתף
בשמחתכם.
אבל ברכותי הטובות לכם שיגדל בנכם
בתורה בחכמה וביראת שמים
מלוה אתכם, דרישת שלום
נחמה ל.

*Above: Nechama Leibowitz's handwritten response and its transcription to our
family's Bar Mitzvah celebration. A translation appears alongside.*

NECHAMA'S SELF-DEFINED

CONTRIBUTION TO TORAH LEARNING

ECHAMA LEIBOWITZ DID NOT VIEW HERSELF AS AN INNOVA-
tor. She defined her role as conveying to the learner the opinions,
often divergent ones, of the commentators. Her goal was to facilitate an understanding of the text and the basis for the varying opinions
approaching the text.

I asked Nechama during one of our phone calls whether she credited
herself with any original contributions to Torah learning. I was referring
to *hiddushim*, novel interpretations. After a brief pause, she answered,
"Charting."

As discussed in the chapter "Pedagogic Principles," Nechama encouraged the careful comparison of texts that may appear to be similar at first,
but contain differences. While these differences are sometimes subtle, they
may convey vital messages. Nechama modeled the role of a teacher as a fa-
cilitator. If the teacher presents the challenge in a clear fashion, the student
can discover the answer through active involvement. When comparing
texts, the mechanism that best highlights similarities and differences is the
chart. Nechama observed that when people read the traditional printed
text and must flip to the second location, it is difficult to detect differences.
The chart, which places the texts side by side, facilitates a quick comparison. Nechama endorsed the use of charts for both children and adults.

An example follows:

The textual example cited in this chapter was presented by Nechama Leibowitz in her
classes on Pedagogy delivered at the CAJE Convention, 5748/1988.

:........... THE BURIAL OF JACOB

Joseph's Request to Pharaoh (Genesis 50:5-6)	Jacob's Charge to Joseph (Genesis 47:29-31)
—	אִם־נָא מָצָאתִי חֵן בְּעֵינֶיךָ
אָבִי הִשְׁבִּיעַנִי לֵאמֹר	שִׂים־נָא יָדְךָ תַּחַת יְרֵכִי
—	וְעָשִׂיתָ עִמָּדִי חֶסֶד וֶאֱמֶת
—	אַל־נָא תִקְבְּרֵנִי בְּמִצְרָיִם
הִנֵּה אָנֹכִי מֵת	וְשָׁכַבְתִּי עִם־אֲבֹתַי
—	וּנְשָׂאתַנִי מִמִּצְרַיִם
בְּקִבְרִי	וּקְבַרְתַּנִי בִּקְבֻרָתָם
אֲשֶׁר כָּרִיתִי לִי	—
בְּאֶרֶץ כְּנַעַן שָׁמָּה תִּקְבְּרֵנִי	—
וַיֹּאמֶר פַּרְעֹה עֲלֵה וּקְבֹר אֶת־אָבִיךָ כַּאֲשֶׁר הִשְׁבִּיעֶךָ	וַיִּשָּׁבַע לוֹ

Joseph's Request to Pharaoh (Genesis 50:5-6)	Jacob's Charge to Joseph (Genesis 47:29-31)
—	Please, if I have found favor in your eyes
My father adjured me saying	Please place your hand under my thigh
—	And do a kindness and truth with me
—	Please do not bury me in Egypt
Behold, I am about to die	For I will lie down with my fathers
—	And you shall transport me out of Egypt
In my grave	And bury me in their tomb
Which I have hewn for myself	—
In the Land of Canaan, there you are to bury me	—
Pharaoh said, "Go up and bury your father as he adjured you"	. . . and he swore to him

What did Joseph add that Jacob did not say? Why?

What did Joseph omit from Jacob's words? Why?

With the key differences between the passages highlighted by the chart, the learner can now explore the meaning of the changes.

PEDAGOGIC PRINCIPLES

N ECHAMA LEIBOWITZ WAS DEDICATED BOTH TO TEACHING
Torah and to guiding others in how to teach Torah. She was an
early advocate of what would later be called, in pedagogic professional literature, active or engaged learning.

In a session led by Nechama Leibowitz at the 1988 CAJE[1] educators'
conference held in Jerusalem, Nechama outlined several of her instructional methodologies designed to promote engagement and understanding. By way of introduction, she noted that in many classes, students are
bored. A primary cause is an overdose of teacher talk. Nechama said, "If a
teacher is speaking eighty percent of the time, this is horrible. The student
must be working most of the time on the text."

Nechama discouraged instructors from teaching in a manner that requires students to take notes. "At Mount Sinai," she said, "there were more
important items and we didn't take notes!" When I studied with Nechama
Leibowitz in class, she often demanded that students put down their writing instruments. I believe that her underlying philosophy was motivated
by her goal to teach methods of learning, even to young students, rather
than the memorization of facts. She wanted students to grapple with the
Torah text, not with their notebooks.

To facilitate active learning, Nechama recommended the strategies which
follow. The list is not meant to be exhaustive; time limits imposed by the
structure of the conference session certainly required Nechama Leibowitz

---

1 Conference for the Advancement of Jewish Education

to limit the items that she presented. Nechama cautioned educators not to use any one method too frequently, creating a predictable pattern.

.... COMPARISON OF NAMES AND APPELLATIONS

At times, the Tanach (comprised of the Bible, Prophets and Writings) uses different names to refer to the same individual(s). Challenging students to break the code in the pattern of usage provides an excellent motivation for learning the chapter or section under study.

Examples of multiple names include:

Example A: Genesis 42:1-6

Jacob saw that there were provisions in Egypt; Jacob said to *his sons*, "Why do you make yourselves seen?" He said, "Behold, I have heard that there are provisions in Egypt. Go down there and buy for us from there [so that] we may live and not die." *Joseph's brothers*, ten of them, went down to buy grain from Egypt. But Benjamin, Joseph's brother, Jacob did not send with his brothers, for he said, "Lest disaster befall him." The *sons of Israel* came to buy provisions among the others who were coming, for the famine was in the Land of Canaan. Joseph was the ruler over the land. He was the provider to all the people of the land. Joseph's brothers came and bowed to him, their faces to the ground.

וַיַּרְא יַעֲקֹב כִּי יֶשׁ־שֶׁבֶר בְּמִצְרָיִם
וַיֹּאמֶר יַעֲקֹב לְבָנָיו לָמָּה תִּתְרָאוּ:
וַיֹּאמֶר הִנֵּה שָׁמַעְתִּי כִּי יֶשׁ־שֶׁבֶר
בְּמִצְרָיִם רְדוּ־שָׁמָּה וְשִׁבְרוּ־לָנוּ
מִשָּׁם וְנִחְיֶה וְלֹא נָמוּת: וַיֵּרְדוּ
אֲחֵי־יוֹסֵף עֲשָׂרָה לִשְׁבֹּר בָּר
מִמִּצְרָיִם: וְאֶת־בִּנְיָמִין אֲחִי יוֹסֵף
לֹא־שָׁלַח יַעֲקֹב אֶת־אֶחָיו כִּי
אָמַר פֶּן־יִקְרָאֶנּוּ אָסוֹן: וַיָּבֹאוּ בְּנֵי
יִשְׂרָאֵל לִשְׁבֹּר בְּתוֹךְ הַבָּאִים כִּי־
הָיָה הָרָעָב בְּאֶרֶץ כְּנָעַן: וְיוֹסֵף הוּא
הַשַּׁלִּיט עַל־הָאָרֶץ הוּא הַמַּשְׁבִּיר
לְכָל־עַם הָאָרֶץ וַיָּבֹאוּ אֲחֵי יוֹסֵף
וַיִּשְׁתַּחֲווּ־לוֹ אַפַּיִם אָרְצָה:

The Torah uses three different terms to identify Jacob's sons. Students should be challenged to explain why each term is appropriate for the context of its usage.

Possible explanations include:

Verse 1: "to his sons" – this is a normal and expected reference to the father-child relationship. Perhaps it also conveys concern for the well-being of the family members. Perhaps it indicates an expectation of Jacob that his sons will fulfill his request.[1]

Verse 3: "Joseph's brothers . . . went down" – "As soon as we reach the subject of Egypt, the biblical record prepares us and them for the meeting with Joseph."[2] Rashi sees this reference as revealing to us that the brothers intended to search for Joseph, redeem him and act with affection to their brother.

This reference of "Joseph's brothers" is used a second time in verse 6.

Now Joseph was the ruler over the land. He was the provider to all the population of the land. Joseph's brothers came and bowed to him with their faces to the ground.	וְיוֹסֵף הוּא הַשַּׁלִּיט עַל־הָאָרֶץ הוּא הַמַּשְׁבִּיר לְכָל־עַם הָאָרֶץ וַיָּבֹאוּ אֲחֵי יוֹסֵף וַיִּשְׁתַּחֲווּ־לוֹ אַפַּיִם אָרְצָה:

Nechama opined that since the act of bowing to Joseph is connected to Joseph's dreams about his brothers from years before, the Torah uses the term "Joseph's brothers" here. Perhaps the first use of this term in verse 3 can also be seen as the Torah setting the stage for events connected to the fulfillment of Joseph's dreams.[3]

Verse 5: "the sons of Israel" – In the international community, Jacob's clan was known as בְּנֵי יִשְׂרָאֵל, the Sons of Israel. As the brothers' arrival was typical of many communities' travel to Egypt with the goal of purchasing food, the text uses the national reference, "sons of Israel."

---

1 These suggestions are the author's opinion.

2 Cited from *Studies in Bereishit*, 462–463.

3 Author's comment.

Example B: Genesis 21:14–21

(This selection may be found in Nechama Leibowitz's weekly gilyonot for Va-yera 5711)

Abraham awoke early in the morning, took bread and a container of water and gave them to Hagar, putting it on her shoulder, and **the child**; he sent her away. She went and wandered in the desert of Be'er Sheva. The water was finished from the container and she cast **the child** under one of the shrubs. She went and sat herself down across, about a bowshot away; for she said, "Let me not see the death of **the child**." She sat across, lifted her voice and wept. God heard the voice of the **youth**; the angel of God called to Hagar from the heavens and said to her, "What ails you, Hagar? Do not fear, for God has heard the voice of **the youth** from where he is. Arise, lift up **the youth** and keep your hand strong on him for I will make him a great nation." God opened her eyes and she saw a well of water. She went and filled the container with water and gave drink to **the youth**. God was with **the youth**; he grew up and lived in the desert and became an archer. He lived in the desert of Paran; his mother took a wife for him from the land of Egypt.

וַיַּשְׁכֵּם אַבְרָהָם בַּבֹּקֶר וַיִּקַּח־לֶחֶם וְחֵמַת מַיִם וַיִּתֵּן אֶל־הָגָר שָׂם עַל־שִׁכְמָהּ וְאֶת־הַיֶּלֶד וַיְשַׁלְּחֶהָ וַתֵּלֶךְ וַתֵּתַע בְּמִדְבַּר בְּאֵר שָׁבַע: וַיִּכְלוּ הַמַּיִם מִן־הַחֵמֶת וַתַּשְׁלֵךְ אֶת־הַיֶּלֶד תַּחַת אַחַד הַשִּׂיחִם: וַתֵּלֶךְ וַתֵּשֶׁב לָהּ מִנֶּגֶד הַרְחֵק כִּמְטַחֲוֵי קֶשֶׁת כִּי אָמְרָה אַל־אֶרְאֶה בְּמוֹת הַיָּלֶד וַתֵּשֶׁב מִנֶּגֶד וַתִּשָּׂא אֶת־קֹלָהּ וַתֵּבְךְּ: וַיִּשְׁמַע אֱלֹהִים אֶת־קוֹל הַנַּעַר וַיִּקְרָא מַלְאַךְ אֱלֹהִים אֶל־הָגָר מִן־הַשָּׁמַיִם וַיֹּאמֶר לָהּ מַה־לָּךְ הָגָר אַל־תִּירְאִי כִּי־שָׁמַע אֱלֹהִים אֶל־קוֹל הַנַּעַר בַּאֲשֶׁר הוּא־שָׁם: קוּמִי שְׂאִי אֶת־הַנַּעַר וְהַחֲזִיקִי אֶת־יָדֵךְ בּוֹ כִּי־לְגוֹי גָּדוֹל אֲשִׂימֶנּוּ: וַיִּפְקַח אֱלֹהִים אֶת־עֵינֶיהָ וַתֵּרֶא בְּאֵר מָיִם וַתֵּלֶךְ וַתְּמַלֵּא אֶת־הַחֵמֶת מַיִם וַתַּשְׁקְ אֶת־הַנָּעַר: וַיְהִי אֱלֹהִים אֶת־הַנַּעַר וַיִּגְדָּל וַיֵּשֶׁב בַּמִּדְבָּר וַיְהִי רֹבֶה קַשָּׁת: וַיֵּשֶׁב בְּמִדְבַּר פָּארָן וַתִּקַּח־לוֹ אִמּוֹ אִשָּׁה מֵאֶרֶץ מִצְרָיִם:

The student is encouraged to study the way Abraham and Hagar refer to Ishmael as יֶלֶד, a child, in contrast to God's and the angel's references to Ishmael as a נַעַר, a youth or young man.

Nechama noted that parents will always view their child as a יֶלֶד (with the connotation of tenderness, connection to, and dependence upon the parent[4]). God and the angel view Ishmael more objectively as "the young man," which he was at age thirteen or older.

---

4 Author's observation.

For further study, one may compare the change from Abraham's ear-lier reference (verse 11) of בְּנוֹ, "his son," to the references of יֶלֶד, "boy."[5] Similarly, Hagar's change from יֶלֶד to נַעַר, which occurs after her encounter with the angel, warrants analysis.[6]

Example C: Genesis 24:61

(This selection may be found in Nechama Leibowitz's weekly gilyonot for Hayyei Sarah 5713)

Rebecca and her maidens arose. They rode upon the camels and went after the man. The servant took Rebecca and went.	וַתָּקָם רִבְקָה וְנַעֲרֹתֶיהָ וַתִּרְכַּבְנָה עַל־הַגְּמַלִּים וַתֵּלַכְנָה אַחֲרֵי הָאִישׁ וַיִּקַּח הָעֶבֶד אֶת־רִבְקָה וַיֵּלַךְ:

The students should be able to identify that the same person, in the same verse, is referred to as both הָאִישׁ ("the man" – carrying the connotation of independence and importance) and הָעֶבֶד ("the servant"). Why?

Nechama noted that it is rare to find different appellations in the same verse. In the above example, each of the two appellations is from a different perspective (i.e., Rebecca and her maidens follow the man, but the man sees himself in the role of Abraham's servant.)

In the following example, one individual refers to a character in two different ways.

Example D: Genesis 34:3

His [Shehem's] soul clung to Dina, daughter of Jacob. He loved the lass and spoke to the lass's heart.	וַתִּדְבַּק נַפְשׁוֹ בְּדִינָה בַּת־יַעֲקֹב וַיֶּאֱהַב אֶת־הַנַּעֲרָ וַיְדַבֵּר עַל־לֵב הַנַּעֲרָ:

Nechama made a brief comment indicating that the "clinging of the soul" carries a spiritual connotation and is employed in conjunction with the

---

5 Nechama endorsed my suggestion that this change reflects a shift in the manner that Abraham related to Ishmael. Now that he has banished his son, Abraham begins to distance himself. "Lad" (*yeled*) is more removed than "son" (*ben*).

6 Author's observation.

reference to Dina being "Jacob's daughter." This author notes the Malbim's commentary:

> Clinging of the soul is possible only when the individuals are from the same socio-economic stratum, as Shehem and Dina were. Shehem was a "prince of the land," and so was Dina, by virtue of being "the daughter of Jacob."[7]

Example E: 2 Samuel 12:1–4
Nathan the prophet, in preparing to rebuke King David, presents a parable.

God sent Nathan to David. He came to him and said to him: "There were two men in one city, one wealthy and one poor. The wealthy one had very many flocks and herds. But the poor one had nothing except one little ewe lamb that he had bought and raised. It grew up together with him and his children; from his bread did it eat and from his cup did it drink and in his bosom it would sleep and was like a daughter to him.

"A traveler came to the rich man, and he spared to take from his own flock and from his own herd for the guest who had come to him. He took the poor man's lamb and prepared it for the man who had come to him."

וַיִּשְׁלַח יְדֹוָה אֶת־נָתָן אֶל־דָּוִד וַיָּבֹא אֵלָיו וַיֹּאמֶר לוֹ שְׁנֵי אֲנָשִׁים הָיוּ בְּעִיר אֶחָת אֶחָד עָשִׁיר וְאֶחָד רָאשׁ: לְעָשִׁיר הָיָה צֹאן וּבָקָר הַרְבֵּה מְאֹד: וְלָרָשׁ אֵין־כֹּל כִּי אִם־כִּבְשָׂה אַחַת קְטַנָּה אֲשֶׁר קָנָה וַיְחַיֶּהָ וַתִּגְדַּל עִמּוֹ וְעִם־בָּנָיו יַחְדָּו מִפִּתּוֹ תֹאכַל וּמִכֹּסוֹ תִשְׁתֶּה וּבְחֵיקוֹ תִשְׁכָּב וַתְּהִי־לוֹ כְּבַת: וַיָּבֹא הֵלֶךְ לְאִישׁ הֶעָשִׁיר וַיַּחְמֹל לָקַחַת מִצֹּאנוֹ וּמִבְּקָרוֹ לַעֲשׂוֹת לָאֹרֵחַ הַבָּא־לוֹ וַיִּקַּח אֶת־כִּבְשַׂת הָאִישׁ הָרָאשׁ וַיַּעֲשֶׂהָ לָאִישׁ הַבָּא אֵלָיו:

The Talmud (*Sukkah* 52b) notes that the last verse includes three different references to the wayfarer. First he is a traveler, just passing by. Then he is a guest who will be lodging with the rich man. Finally, he becomes "the

---

7 See also Genesis 34:4. וַיֹּאמֶר שְׁכֶם אֶל־חֲמוֹר אָבִיו לֵאמֹר קַח־לִי אֶת־הַיַּלְדָּה הַזֹּאת לְאִשָּׁה:
Shehem said to Hamor, his father, saying: "Take this girl for me as a wife."
Here, Shehem refers to Dina as a יַלְדָּה, girl; in the previous verse, twice he identifies Dina as a נַעֲרָה, a lass or young lady. A יַלְדָּה, girl, is a minor. The term appears to belittle Dina and reflect a right to make decisions for her without her consent (author's observation).

man," as if he himself were the head of the household! The traveler is a metaphor, representing the *yetzer ha-ra*, the evil inclination. Once we open the door, it quickly takes over. Nechama suggested this source as a good parable to warn against starting bad habits such as smoking and drug use.

Example F: I Kings

Now King David was old, advanced in years; they covered him with clothes, but he could not become warm. (I Kings 1:1)	וְהַמֶּלֶךְ דָּוִד זָקֵן בָּא בַּיָּמִים וַיְכַסֻּהוּ בַּבְּגָדִים וְלֹא יִחַם לוֹ:

David's days drew near to die. He charged Solomon his son, saying . . . . (I Kings 2:1)	וַיִּקְרְבוּ יְמֵי־דָוִד לָמוּת וַיְצַו אֶת־ שְׁלֹמֹה בְנוֹ לֵאמֹר:

Students should be challenged first to identify the difference in the way the text refers to King David. In Kings 2:1, the title "King" is not used. Second, to explain why. Perhaps they will propose the Talmud's observation that "There is no kingship on the day of death." Indeed, King David died on that very day, as recorded in 2:10:

David slept with his forefathers; he was buried in the City of David.	וַיִּשְׁכַּב דָּוִד עִם־אֲבֹתָיו וַיִּקָּבֵר בְּעִיר דָּוִד:

:........... COMPARISON OF SIMILAR TEXTS
:
:

Nechama Leibowitz noted that at times, a student may know all the facts of an episode and still not have a full understanding of the material and its meaning. Guiding students to compare similar yet different textual references stimulates their motivation to learn, deepens their comprehension and increases their appreciation of the subtle messages contained in the biblical passages.

Example A: Genesis 24

In Eliezer's search to identify a suitable wife for Isaac, he designs a test presented in verse 14:

| It shall be that the young woman to whom I shall say "Please tip your jug that I may drink," and she will say, "Drink, and I will also draw water for your camels" – she is the one that You have designated for my master, for Isaac, and through her I will know that You have done kindness with my master." | וְהָיָה הַנַּעֲרָ אֲשֶׁר אֹמַר אֵלֶיהָ הַטִּי־נָא כַדֵּךְ וְאֶשְׁתֶּה וְאָמְרָה שְׁתֵה וְגַם־גְּמַלֶּיךָ אַשְׁקֶה אֹתָהּ הֹכַחְתָּ לְעַבְדְּךָ לְיִצְחָק וּבָהּ אֵדַע כִּי־עָשִׂיתָ חֶסֶד עִם־אֲדֹנִי: |

During the actual encounter, the Torah states in verses 18–19:

| 18. She said, "Drink, my master." She quickly lowered her jug onto her hand and gave him drink. 19. She finished giving him drink and said, "Also for your camels I will draw water until they have finished drinking." | (יח) וַתֹּאמֶר שְׁתֵה אֲדֹנִי וַתְּמַהֵר וַתֹּרֶד כַּדָּהּ עַל־יָדָהּ וַתַּשְׁקֵהוּ: (יט) וַתְּכַל לְהַשְׁקֹתוֹ וַתֹּאמֶר גַּם לִגְמַלֶּיךָ אֶשְׁאָב עַד אִם־כִּלּוּ לִשְׁתֹּת: |

How does Rebecca's response in verse 18 differ from the answer the servant suggested would confirm that she was the designated spouse for Isaac? What does this tell us about Rebecca?

What changes from the servant's plan are recorded in verse 19?[8]

(See the chapter "Nechama's Self-Defined Contribution to Torah Learning" for an additional example of similar, but different, texts presented during this class. The chapter highlights Nechama Leibowitz's view that the most effective way to compare similar verses is through the use of a chart.)

Example B: Genesis 24:28/29:12

After Eliezer bestows gifts upon Rebecca, he inquires about her lineage and asks whether there are accommodations in her father's house. Rebecca answers, and Eliezer thanks God for guiding him to his master's relatives.

---

8 Author's question.

Then, the Torah tells us:

The maiden ran and told her mother's household about these events.

וַתָּרָץ הַנַּעֲרָ וַתַּגֵּד לְבֵית אִמָּהּ כַּדְּבָרִים הָאֵלֶּה:

Years later, when Jacob introduces himself to Rachel at the well, the Torah tells us:

Jacob told Rachel that he was her father's brother and that he was Rebecca's son. She ran and told her father.

וַיַּגֵּד יַעֲקֹב לְרָחֵל כִּי אֲחִי אָבִיהָ הוּא וְכִי בֶן־רִבְקָה הוּא וַתָּרָץ וַתַּגֵּד לְאָבִיהָ:

Which parent does each of our future matriarchs choose to tell of her encounter? Why does Rachel tell her father while Rebecca told her mother?

The Ramban suggests that the natural person to whom to report is the father. In both cases, it was a relative of the father who either appeared or was represented. Therefore, it should be he who goes out to honor the guest. Further, it was the father who, in biblical times, would be responsible to bring the visitor into his house and to provide the food.

Why then did Rebecca run to her mother? Because she had received a gift of jewelry. Rebecca was eager to show her present to her mother, as was customary for young women.

Example C: Genesis 6–8

Sometimes, when God gives a command with several parts, we find that the fulfillment is partial and/or completed in a different order. For example, God tells Noah:

I will establish my covenant with you and you shall enter the ark; you, your sons, your wife and your sons' wives with you. (Genesis 6:18)

וַהֲקִמֹתִי אֶת־בְּרִיתִי אִתָּךְ וּבָאתָ אֶל־הַתֵּבָה אַתָּה וּבָנֶיךָ וְאִשְׁתְּךָ וּנְשֵׁי־בָנֶיךָ אִתָּךְ:

Noah does so, as we find in Genesis 7:7:

Noah and his sons, his wife, and his sons' wives went with him to the ark because of the flood waters.	וַיָּבֹא נֹחַ וּבָנָיו וְאִשְׁתּוֹ וּנְשֵׁי־בָנָיו אִתּוֹ אֶל־הַתֵּבָה מִפְּנֵי מֵי הַמַּבּוּל:

However, at the conclusion of the Flood, God commands Noah:

Leave the ark, you and your wife and your sons and your sons' wives with you. (Genesis 8:16)	צֵא מִן־הַתֵּבָה אַתָּה וְאִשְׁתְּךָ וּבָנֶיךָ וּנְשֵׁי־בָנֶיךָ אִתָּךְ:

What does Noah do?

Noah departed and his sons, and his wife and his sons' wives with him. (Genesis 8:18)	וַיֵּצֵא־נֹחַ וּבָנָיו וְאִשְׁתּוֹ וּנְשֵׁי־בָנָיו אִתּוֹ:

Noah leaves the ark as he entered it, but not as God commanded. Why?

Rashi (Genesis 6:18 and 7:7) explains that the men and women were commanded to enter the ark separately and not to engage in marital relations, as the world was in distress. When the Flood is over, God permits marital relations once again, as we see reflected in the command for Noah to leave with his wife and his sons with their wives (see Rashi on 8:16). Apparently, in the wake of the destruction, Noah was not ready to resume the full spectrum of married life.

.... COMPARISON OF COMMENTATORS
:
:

One of Nechama's main methodologies was to compare the differing opinions of the commentators. Her weekly gilyonot (study sheets) are replete with the challenge to identify the basis for multiple views. Her published studies on the weekly Torah portions also contain many explorations of the commentators' divergent opinions. (Nechama acknowledged that this type of exercise can be time-consuming.)

Example: Genesis 46:29

Joseph harnessed his chariot and went up to meet his father in Goshen. He appeared before him, he fell on his neck and wept on his neck excessively.

וַיֶּאְסֹר יוֹסֵף מֶרְכַּבְתּוֹ וַיַּעַל לִקְרַאת־
יִשְׂרָאֵל אָבִיו גֹּשְׁנָה וַיֵּרָא אֵלָיו וַיִּפֹּל
עַל־צַוָּארָיו וַיֵּבְךְּ עַל־צַוָּארָיו עוֹד:

RASHI: Joseph appeared to his father and he wept a great amount, more than customary. But Jacob did not fall on Joseph's neck, nor did he kiss him. Our sages say that he [Jacob] was reciting the Shema.

RAMBAN: I do not understand why the Torah includes "he appeared before him." This is understood once we are told that he fell upon his neck. Furthermore, it is not respectful for Joseph to fall upon his father's neck. Rather, he should prostrate himself or kiss his hand, as is it recorded: Joseph then removed them from his knees and prostrated himself with his face toward the ground. (Genesis 48:12)

. . . The correct explanation, in my opinion, is that Yisrael's [Jacob's] vision was somewhat weakened from his advanced age, and when Joseph approached in the royal chariot with the headdress that Egyptian rulers customarily wore, he was not recognizable to his father, nor did his brothers recognize him. Therefore, the text tells us that when he appeared before his father, he [Jacob] looked at him, recognized him, and then his father fell upon his neck and wept upon him exceedingly . . . . Afterwards, he said, "I can now die after having seen your face."

It is a known fact by whom tears are found; is it by the aged father who finds his son alive after despair and mourning, or is it by the young son who rules?

What is the basis for the differing opinions as to which one fell upon the neck of the other? (The reader is encouraged to take some time to ponder this question. A rereading of the verse is recommended.)

Nechama Leibowitz's analysis:

Rashi takes a linguistic approach.[9] The identified subject in the verse is Joseph. All verbs which follow are connected to this predicate until a new subject is introduced. Hence, it is Joseph who prepared his chariot, it is Joseph who went up and appeared to Jacob and it is Joseph who fell upon the neck of his father.

The Ramban, explained Nechama, looks at the episode from a psychological perspective. Who is more likely to burst into tears? It is the aged father who had thought that his son was dead.

.... ## USE OF MIDRASH

Nechama Leibowitz endorsed the use of Midrash, but with careful application. One must be selective in deciding which Midrash to teach, the manner in which to teach it and the age of students to whom it is taught.

Midrash often identifies a character of one era with a character from a

---

9 I asked Nechama Leibowitz if this linguistic approach was a consistent rule in Rashi's commentary. After all, by the sale of Joseph, Rashi does not adhere to this same guideline. The Torah relates:

They sat down to eat bread and raised their eyes and saw — behold, there was a caravan of Ishmaelites coming from Gilad and their camels were carrying spices, balsam and lotus, traveling to bring them down to Egypt. Judah said to his brothers, "What gain will there be if we kill our brother and conceal his blood? Come, let us sell him to the Ishmaelites, and let our hand not be upon him for he is our brother, our flesh." His brothers agreed. Midianite men, traders, passed by. They drew Joseph up and lifted him out of the pit, and they sold Joseph to the Ishmaelites for twenty silver pieces. They brought Joseph to Egypt. (Genesis 37:25–28)

If Rashi were to apply the linguistic approach here as he did with the meeting of Joseph and his father, he should have concluded, as the Rashbam states, that the Midianite merchants were the ones who removed Joseph from the pit while the brothers were still eating. However, Rashi's opinion is that the brothers were the ones who raised Joseph from the pit and sold him to the Ishmaelites, who in turn sold him to the Midianites, who were also traveling in the area.

Nechama explained that Rashi does not operate with a fixed linguistic rule. He judges the meaning by the full context. Since the brothers agreed to Judah's plan to sell Joseph (verse 27), they are the subject of the phrase, "They pulled and raised Joseph from the pit." To support Rashi's opinion, Nechama cited Joseph's declaration: ". . . I am Joseph your brother, whom you sold to Egypt" (Genesis 45:4).

different time. For example, the Midrash states that the donkey that ac-
companied Abraham and Isaac on the journey to Mount Moriah was the
same one that Moses used to transport his wife and children to Egypt. The
same donkey will also carry the Messiah when he arrives. This type of
Midrash should not be taught to children younger than fourth grade.

On the other hand, some midrashic selections are crucial to understanding the text. The episode of Sodom and its environs requires input from
the Midrash. How could entire cities be destroyed? The Midrash provides
the background. (Nechama noted that these midrashic selections are based
on Ezekiel 16.)

Some teachers shy away from Midrash because they argue that children
are not able to differentiate what is the Torah text and what is Midrash.
Nechama said, "This is not the worst thing. At least they will know something. Is this a Jewish tragedy? Over this I would not cry."[10]

When students study Midrash, they should be given an exercise that will
prompt their understanding. A primary question should be: What does the
selected Midrash add to the content of the verse that we are now studying? Nechama discouraged asking students to summarize or paraphrase the
Midrash. She wanted them to interact with the selection (this held true
for the Torah text, as well) process their knowledge and use it to answer a
question in a way that would show that they had assimilated the material.

Example: Midrash Tanhuma, Parashat Toldot, Chapter 5
The Haftarah selection for the portion of Noah includes Isaiah 54:17. It
reads as follows:

No weapon formed against you shall prosper, and   כָּל־כְּלִי יוּצַר עָלַיִךְ לֹא יִצְלָח
any tongue that rises against you in judgment you   וְכָל־לָשׁוֹן תָּקוּם־אִתָּךְ לַמִּשְׁפָּט

---

10 This author believes that it is vital that the teacher know what is actually in the
Torah text and what our sages added in the Midrash, and that students be told when an
opinion comes from the Midrash. If they do not remember the distinction in a particu-
lar instance, at least they will have acquired an appreciation of the concept of Midrash
supplementing the information provided directly in the text. Perhaps this was Nechama
Leibowitz's intention.

shall condemn. This is the heritage of the servants of God, and their righteousness is from Me, says God. תַּרְשִׁיעִי זֹאת נַחֲלַת עַבְדֵי יְ־הֹוָה
וְצִדְקָתָם מֵאִתִּי נְאֻם־יְ־הֹוָה:

The Midrash says:

> You find the Jewish people saying before the Holy One, Blessed be He, "Master of the Universe, see how the idol worshipers enslave us. They have no other work; rather, they sit and conspire against us." God answered them: "What success do they have? They enact decrees against you and I annul and destroy them." As it is stated . . . Pharaoh commanded his entire nation, saying, "Every son that is born, you shall throw into the river" (Exodus 1:22). But the Holy Spirit shouts, "Who is he that says and it comes to pass when the Lord commands it not?" (Lamentations 3:37) Pharaoh commanded, but God did not command. Rather, the more that they afflicted them, the more they multiplied and grew" (Exodus 1:12). Haman sought to destroy all the Jews, but God did not seek that. It was turned to the contrary, that the Jews had dominion... (Esther 9:1). Balak and Bilam sought to curse the Jews, but God did not seek that. As it is said, "But the Lord thy God would not hearken to Bilam" (Deuteronomy 23:6). Therefore, it is written, "Who is he that says and it comes to pass when the Lord commands it not?" (Lamentations 3:37). This is [the meaning of the verse] "No weapon formed against you shall prosper."

One of the questions Nechama would ask regarding this Midrash, in order to promote review and understanding, is: Why does the Midrash refer to the enemies of the Jews in non-chronological order (placing Haman before Balak and Bilam)? Her answer was that the Midrash sees Pharaoh and Haman as examples of "No *weapon* formed against you shall prosper," while Balak and Bilam are examples of the verse, "Any tongue that rises against you in judgment shall you condemn."

Nechama Leibowitz was an avid proponent and practitioner of asking students to jot down their answers to the instructor's question. When each pupil or *havruta* (member of a study pair) must write an answer, all are involved simultaneously. When I studied in class with Nechama, several times in the same lesson she would require all twenty-five students to write their answers. She would either rotate among us or call students to her desk so that she could check every answer.

I believe that on another occasion, Nechama Leibowitz shared the belief that only when one can express his thoughts clearly in writing is he able to demonstrate full comprehension.

★

Nechama said that when designing learning activities to promote student involvement, thinking and understanding, it is not necessary to first teach a chapter or large block of verses. Exploration may begin almost immediately. On other occasions, Nechama also cautioned against learning individual verses in isolation without appreciating the context of the story.

Nechama often said that students love to think. The above methodologies will aid the teacher in stimulating thinking and engagement.

★

Some of the questions presented in this chapter have been left unanswered. There are two reasons for this:

1. Nechama did not provide an answer during this presentation, and I refrained from including my own thoughts.
2. In tribute to Nechama Leibowitz, some questions are left for the reader to ponder and suggest possible answers. Nechama Leibowitz encouraged learners to think on their own and not to rely on her answers.

See the chapter "I Ask Questions" for an elaboration on this trait of Nechama Leibowitz.

ON TEACHING HUMASH IN THE DIASPORA

D URING A TELEPHONE CONVERSATION IN MAY 1994 (SIVAN 5754), Nechama Leibowitz shared a succinct view of how to teach – and how not to teach – Humash to students whose primary language is one other than Hebrew.

The essential preliminary skill required for proficient and meaningful Torah study is knowledge of Hebrew. To study Torah in the original, a vocabulary fund of three hundred to eight hundred[1] words is necessary. Nechama endorsed establishing the curricular focus of first grade as language acquisition. She believed that it was possible for first-grade Diaspora students to learn as many as six hundred words. Once pupils acquire this fund of words, it is possible to teach Humash in Hebrew without the need for ongoing translation.[2]

When the formal study of Humash begins (usually in second grade[3]), its

---

From conversations with Nechama Leibowitz on 4 Elul 5753/August 21, 1993 and 19 Sivan 5754/May 29, 1994.

1 The upper range is not legible in my notes. However, after discussing this topic in July 2007 with Professor Haramati, a colleague and friend of Professor Leibowitz, it appears that eight hundred is accurate.

2 In a conversation with Nechama in her apartment on 5 Elul 5753 (August 21, 1993), she noted that she had been teaching for fifty years. In her experience, she has found that "a student who studied [Humash] in Hebrew can be taught everything. One who studied in English – it's difficult to teach him."

3 Nechama recommended starting the formal study of Humash with Parashat Lech Lecha.

focus should be on content. Nechama advocated learning for meaning, not just for recall of facts.

For example, when teaching Abraham's welcoming of the three guests, the teacher should write the appropriate phrases on the board and help the students to observe the differences between Abraham's words and his actions.

המעשה (בראשית יח:ו-ח)	דברי אברהם (בראשית יח:ה)
וַיְמַהֵר אַבְרָהָם הָאֹהֱלָה אֶל־שָׂרָה	—
וַיֹּאמֶר מַהֲרִי שְׁלֹשׁ סְאִים קֶמַח סֹלֶת לוּשִׁי וַעֲשִׂי עֻגוֹת	וְאֶקְחָה פַת־לֶחֶם
וַיֹּאכֵלוּ (פסוק ח')	וְסַעֲדוּ לִבְּכֶם אַחַר תַּעֲבֹרוּ
וְאֶל־הַבָּקָר רָץ אַבְרָהָם	—
וַיִּקַּח בֶּן־בָּקָר רַךְ וָטוֹב וַיִּתֵּן אֶל־הַנַּעַר וַיְמַהֵר לַעֲשׂוֹת אֹתוֹ	—
וַיִּקַּח חֶמְאָה וְחָלָב וּבֶן־הַבָּקָר אֲשֶׁר עָשָׂה וַיִּתֵּן לִפְנֵיהֶם	—
וְהוּא עֹמֵד עֲלֵיהֶם תַּחַת הָעֵץ	—

Abraham's Offer	**The Actions**
(Genesis 18:5)	(Genesis 18:6–8)
—	Abraham hurried to the tent, to Sarah.
and I will take a piece of bread	He said, "Hurry and prepare three seah [approximately seven pounds] of meal, fine flour. Knead and make cakes."
so that you may satisfy your heart's [appetite]	they ate (verse 8)
—	Abraham ran to the cattle. He took a tender and choice calf
—	he gave it to the lad
—	he hurried to prepare it.
—	He took butter and milk and the calf that he prepared and placed these before them
—	he was standing over them beneath the tree

A discussion should ensue. What are the differences? Why did Abraham do more than he promised?

Other questions about this episode which should be explored with the students include:

- Why did Abraham invite his guests to sit under a tree and not some other place?
- Why, if Abraham was weak, did he run to the travelers?
- Why did Abraham extend himself for non-Jews?

Nechama also allowed for the option to add some Aggada (rabbinic legends) to the young child's study of Torah.

Nechama Leibowitz frowned upon the way Humash is often taught. "It is not good," she said, if the translation of words occupies a significant part of instructional time. She discouraged just reading one verse after another. It is possible to skip verses, even entire chapters (such as the story of Lot and his daughters) in order to focus on understanding the Torah's messages. She saw limited value in asking "Who said to whom" questions and was opposed to assigning questions whose answers could be copied directly from the Humash.

Nechama Leibowitz was dedicated to promoting her students' thinking, which in turn promotes a deeper love for the Torah and its application to the lives of those who study it.

A CLASSIC EXAMPLE

A Gilayon from Nechama Leibowitz
on the Binding of Isaac

FOR THIRTY YEARS – FROM 1941 TO 1971 – NECHAMA LEIBOWITZ issued a weekly sheet presenting thought-provoking questions on the Torah portion and the classical commentators. At times, her questions prompt a deeper understanding of the text and its messages. At other times, her questions develop a keener awareness of the technical skills needed to properly approach the Torah or her commentators.

Nechama Leibowitz was a tenacious proponent of the power of a question. She believed that skillfully crafted questions empower learners to discover truths in the Torah while developing a love for Torah study. As a general rule, Nechama would not provide prepared answers to her questions. She feared that once the answer was readily available in print, the learner would not invest the energy to struggle in thought. While in the short-term the printed answer may provide information, it usually does not facilitate the acquisition of methodological skills, nor does it allow for the full engagement of the individual in the thought process. As such, Nechama insisted that anyone who wanted to know her answer (and most questions have multiple plausible answers) write to her – preferably with his or her own answer. Nechama would then answer in writing, usually marking her responses in red ink. In class, at Beit Midrash L'Torah, she once explained her system of abbreviations. The Hebrew letter נ is נכון (cor-

---

From correspondence with Nechama Leibowitz dated Heshvan 5752 / November 1991 and phone conversation on 1 Shevat 5752/January 6, 1992.

rect); נ.ל. is לא נכון (incorrect) and ל.נ., she said with a smile on her face, is Nechama Leibowitz!

At times, Nechama Leibowitz would jot down a subjective evaluation of one's submitted thoughts, e.g. יפה (nice) or יפה מאוד (very nice). Often she would elaborate, explain why the writer erred in thought, or she would provide an answer where the correspondent produced none. Scores of people from around the world invested hours in order to answer a single gilayon. What was, at times, a difficult handwriting to decipher was attributed to Nechama's reviewing of the responses during a cab ride as she shuttled between the many schools, kibbutzim, and other places where she taught Torah.

In 1963, departing from her policy, Nechama Leibowitz released a volume containing one full year of gilyonot with answers to most (but not all) of the questions she posed. I brought this book with me on a visit to Nechama in 1990 to ask that she inscribe it. Nechama told me that she regretted publishing the volume for the reasons presented above. I offered some justifications for its value and asked whether she had considered recording her answers and storing them away from public access. She told me that her husband had suggested the same, to which she had replied (on the premise that the answers were for her reference only), "What, I won't remember the basis for the difference of opinion between Rashi and Ramban?" "Now," she continued, "I'm getting older and do not remember all my answers." In truth, Nechama's questions remain more important than a recorded answer.

To provide the flavor of the gilyonot, the exchange between this student and the master, and an appreciation of some of the thoughts of Nechama Leibowitz, I present below page one of Nechama's questions from gilayon Va-yera 5715 (1954) focusing on the Binding of Isaac (Genesis 22). In an effort to honor Nechama's goal to promote thinking, the answers appear only after all the questions. The reader is encouraged to tackle the questions on his or her own prior to consulting the answers.

In her earlier gilyonot, including the one below, Nechama Leibowitz provided few quotes from the Torah text and commentators. The learner would consult the sources directly. In later years, Nechama designed the gilyonot to be inclusive of almost all the sources required to tackle the questions posed. The appropriate sources have been added for the reader's benefit. (Please note that an asterisk indicates a difficult question and a double asterisk indicates a very difficult question. Both are the designations of Nechama Leibowitz.)

·········· STUDY SHEETS ON THE WEEKLY PORTION

Edited by Nechama Leibowitz, Fourteenth Year
Published by the Institute for Torah and Education for Adults and Youth
of the Mizrachi Women's Organization of America
Special edition for the World Zionist Organization
Department of Torah Education and Culture in the Diaspora

·········· VA-YERA (5715/1954), CHAPTER 22:
THE AKEDA (THE BINDING)

A.   Questions on Structure and Style

1. It happened after these things that God tested Abraham and said to him, "Abraham," and he said, "Here I am."

(א) וַיְהִי אַחַר הַדְּבָרִים הָאֵלֶּה וְהָאֱלֹהִים נִסָּה אֶת־אַבְרָהָם וַיֹּאמֶר אֵלָיו אַבְרָהָם וַיֹּאמֶר הִנֵּנִי:

2. He said, "Please take your son, your only one, whom you love, Isaac, and go to the Land of Moriah and bring him up there for an offering upon one of the mountains which I shall tell you."

(ב) וַיֹּאמֶר קַח־נָא אֶת־בִּנְךָ אֶת־יְחִידְךָ אֲשֶׁר־אָהַבְתָּ אֶת־יִצְחָק וְלֶךְ־לְךָ אֶל־אֶרֶץ הַמֹּרִיָּה וְהַעֲלֵהוּ שָׁם לְעֹלָה עַל אַחַד הֶהָרִים אֲשֶׁר אֹמַר אֵלֶיךָ:

3. Abraham arose early in the morning, saddled his donkey and took his two lads with him and Isaac his son; he split the wood for an offering, rose up and went to the place the Lord had told him. (Genesis 22:1–3)

(ג) וַיַּשְׁכֵּם אַבְרָהָם בַּבֹּקֶר וַיַּחֲבֹשׁ אֶת־חֲמֹרוֹ וַיִּקַּח אֶת־שְׁנֵי נְעָרָיו אִתּוֹ וְאֵת יִצְחָק בְּנוֹ וַיְבַקַּע עֲצֵי עֹלָה וַיָּקָם וַיֵּלֶךְ אֶל־הַמָּקוֹם אֲשֶׁר־אָמַר־לוֹ הָאֱלֹהִים:

1. Abraham's response in verse 1 comes between two statements by God, but no answer from Abraham, our patriarch, is forthcoming after God's second statement. Explain why.

2. Verses 6–8:

6. Abraham took the wood for the offering and placed it on Isaac, his son. He took in his hand the fire and the knife and the two of them went together.

וַיִּקַּח אַבְרָהָם אֶת־עֲצֵי הָעֹלָה (ו)
וַיָּשֶׂם עַל־יִצְחָק בְּנוֹ וַיִּקַּח בְּיָדוֹ
אֶת־הָאֵשׁ וְאֶת־הַמַּאֲכֶלֶת וַיֵּלְכוּ
שְׁנֵיהֶם יַחְדָּו:

7. Isaac spoke to Abraham his father. He said, "Father." He said, "Here I am, my son." He said, "Here are the fire and the wood, but where is the lamb for the offering?"

וַיֹּאמֶר יִצְחָק אֶל־אַבְרָהָם אָבִיו (ז)
וַיֹּאמֶר אָבִי וַיֹּאמֶר הִנֶּנִּי בְנִי וַיֹּאמֶר
הִנֵּה הָאֵשׁ וְהָעֵצִים וְאַיֵּה הַשֶּׂה
לְעֹלָה:

8. Abraham said, "The Lord will seek out for Himself the lamb for the offering, my son," and the two of them went together. (Genesis 22:6–8)

וַיֹּאמֶר אַבְרָהָם אֱ־לֹהִים (ח)
יִרְאֶה־לּוֹ הַשֶּׂה לְעֹלָה בְּנִי וַיֵּלְכוּ
שְׁנֵיהֶם יַחְדָּו:

Question: The conversation between Abraham and Isaac (verses 7–8 above), the only one in the chapter, comes between two identical phrases, between the double reference of "the two of them went together."

What is the significance of this repetition, and why is this phrase positioned specifically before and after the conversation (between Abraham and Isaac)?

3. Pay attention to one small detail in the conversation between Abraham and Isaac:

Verse 7: He said,   "My father."
         He said,   "Here I am, my son."
         He said,   "Here are the fire and the wood, but where is
                        the lamb for the offering?"

Verse 8: Abraham said, "The Lord will seek out for himself the lamb
                        for the offering, my son," and the two of
                        them went together.

Can you find the reason why Scripture added the name "Abraham" at the end, which is not consistent with the pattern of the Torah?[2]

B. Questions and Analyses in Rashi
(See verses quoted in Question A1)

1. Rashi: "Your son" – he replied to Him, "I have two sons." He [God] said, "Your only son." He said, "This is the only son of his mother and this is the only son of his mother." He said, "The one whom you love." He said, "Both of them I love." He said, "Isaac." And why did He not reveal this [that Isaac was the one to whom God referred] from the outset? In order not to confuse him suddenly lest his mind become distracted and disordered. And in order to endear upon him the command and to give him reward for each and every statement.

(a) What is bothering Rashi in our verse?

**(b) The author of *Be'er Isaac*, a commentary on Rashi, remarks that Rashi provides two contradictory answers to resolve his questions. Explain the contradiction and how they can coexist. (See also Ramban on "Please take your son.")

2. Arose early (22:3)

Abraham arose early in the morning, saddled his donkey and took his two lads with him and Isaac his son; he split the wood for an offering, rose up and went to the place the Lord had told him.

וַיַּשְׁכֵּם אַבְרָהָם בַּבֹּקֶר וַיַּחֲבֹשׁ אֶת־חֲמֹרוֹ וַיִּקַּח אֶת־שְׁנֵי נְעָרָיו אִתּוֹ וְאֵת יִצְחָק בְּנוֹ וַיְבַקַּע עֲצֵי עֹלָה וַיָּקָם וַיֵּלֶךְ אֶל־הַמָּקוֹם אֲשֶׁר־אָמַר־לוֹ הָאֱלֹהִים:

Rashi: "Arose early" – He hastened to observe the commandment. Compare Rashi's comment here (above) to that of the Radak on 21:14. Chapter 21 verse 14 states:

---

2 See the chapter "The Bud Vase" above for an elaboration on the usual pattern of the Torah. See also the chapter "Inner Thoughts Revealed," which discusses verses which, in an explanatory note, Nechama Leibowitz referred to as helpful in answering this question.

Abraham arose early in the morning, he took bread and a skin of water, gave them to Hagar, placed them on her shoulder with the boy and sent her away; she went and strayed in the desert of Be'er Sheva.

וַיַּשְׁכֵּם אַבְרָהָם בַּבֹּקֶר וַיִּקַּח־לֶחֶם וְחֵמַת מַיִם וַיִּתֵּן אֶל־הָגָר שָׂם עַל־שִׁכְמָהּ וְאֶת־הַיֶּלֶד וַיְשַׁלְּחֶהָ וַתֵּלֶךְ וַתֵּתַע בְּמִדְבַּר בְּאֵר שָׁבַע:

Radak: "He arose early" – To fulfill the Divine command.

Question: Can you explain why Rashi did not comment on verse 21:14 in similar fashion to his comment on our verse (22:3) and as indeed the Radak does comment?

3. Verse 5 in our chapter states:

Abraham said to his lads, "Stay here by yourselves with the donkey; I and the lad will go until so (כֹּה) and we will worship and we will return to you."

וַיֹּאמֶר אַבְרָהָם אֶל־נְעָרָיו שְׁבוּ־לָכֶם פֹּה עִם־הַחֲמוֹר וַאֲנִי וְהַנַּעַר נֵלְכָה עַד־כֹּה וְנִשְׁתַּחֲוֶה וְנָשׁוּבָה אֲלֵיכֶם:

"Until so (כֹּה)" – This means a short distance to the place which is ahead of us. The Midrash Aggadah says: "I shall see where is that which God said to me "so (כֹּה) will be your descendants." [This is a reference to Genesis 15:5: He (God) brought him outside and said: "Look now at the heavens and count the stars if you are able to count them.' He said to him, 'So (כֹּה) shall be your offspring.'"]

(a) What difficulty is Rashi addressing?

**(b) Why was Rashi not satisfied with the literal explanation (the first opinion) and added the Midrash Aggadah?

(c) Explain the concept which is symbolized in the words of this Midrash Aggadah.

.... SUGGESTED ANSWERS

(Unless indicated otherwise, the answers below are those suggested by this author. Nechama Leibowitz's comments and alternate suggestions are indicated by her initials, NL.)

A.   Questions on Structure and Style

1. The second statement of God is a command to action. Therefore, Abraham does not respond verbally, but in action. (NL : נ – correct)

    This author asked: Is it accurate to say that Abraham did not respond at all verbally? Or is it possible that he answered, but Scripture only records Abraham's action in order to emphasize that the appropriate response to a Divine command is action?

    NL : *What are you saying? What Abraham did or did not do – of this we know nothing. We are dealing with what is written in our Torah. The question is: why does the Torah convey this episode in this fashion, concluding the conversation after [God says] "which I will tell you"? I think that if the Torah had told us, "All right" or "I will do as you say" or something similar, this would corrupt the magnificent artistry of this story.*

2. The significance of repeating the phrase "the two of them went together" is to inform us that even after Isaac became aware that he might be the sacrifice, he still marched on united with his father, prepared to accept the Divine command. He had the same attachment to his father and the same degree of happiness as he did before this new awareness. (These comments are based on Rashi's commentary.)

    If one holds the opinion that Isaac did not understand that he was to be the offering, then the repeated phrase might be understood to tell us that Isaac trusted in God just as Abraham trusted that God would provide an animal for the sacrifice. (NL : טוב מאוד / very good)

    NL : *This is to say: Scripture repeats the phrase to show us that nothing changed!! We only hear about their steps, moving onward, onward, onward.*

3. It appears to me that when a challenge requires a special effort, the Torah includes the name of the subject to emphasize that he employed his unique strengths in the fulfillment of the challenge. This implies that it was somewhat difficult for Abraham to respond to his son's inquiry. Therefore, he rose to the occasion by summoning the strengths that were characteristic of Abraham. (NL : יפה מאוד / very nice)

NL: *Nice response. Furthermore, Abraham is thinking about his answer; he hesitates. He doesn't answer immediately, which would have been indicated by the Torah stating: He said: God will seek out . . . . Rather, Abraham ponders what he should say to Isaac. The pause is represented by elongating the introductory phrase to say "Abraham said"* [which is two words in Hebrew: וַיֹּאמֶר אַבְרָהָם – ed.] *instead of the usual "he said"* [which is one word in Hebrew: וַיֹּאמֶר – ed.].

By elongating the introductory phrase the Torah slows the pace of the narrative and heightens the drama.

NL: *Excellent. This exactly what I intended [to convey in my comment above.]*

Question submitted by the author: When Isaac speaks to Abraham in verse 7, his words are introduced by "Isaac said to Abraham his father." But when Abraham answers the main question ("Where is the lamb?"), his words are introduced merely by "Abraham said." There is a lack of parallelism as the Torah does not say "Abraham said to his son" or "Abraham, his father, said." What is the significance of this?

At first, Nechama Leibowitz answered that it was not significant as it is not the usual style of the Torah to say: "Abraham, his father, said." It would be superfluous to add the appellative. However, from Isaac's perspective, the appellation "his father" is most understandable. Isaac, who has doubt and fear, turns to one in whom he can find shelter – that is, Abraham in the role of father.

I noted to Nechama Leibowitz that we do have an example of the appellative used by a father in Genesis 27:32:

Isaac, his father, said to him, "Who are you?"	וַיֹּאמֶר לוֹ יִצְחָק אָבִיו מִי־אָתָּה
He said, "I am your firstborn son, Esav."	וַיֹּאמֶר אֲנִי בִּנְךָ בְכֹרְךָ עֵשָׂו:

Nechama subsequently agreed that the lack of parallelism in the Torah's introduction of each comment carries a message. She accepted my suggestion that as Abraham came closer to the anticipated sacrifice of Isaac, he began to distance himself emotionally from his son. We are clued into this change by the absence of the parallelism, by the fact that the Torah states "Abraham said" and not "Abraham, his father, said" or "Abraham said to his son."

Alternately, Nechama proposed the absence of a term that refers to the familial relationship between Abraham and Isaac may reflect that at that moment, Abraham was focused on fulfilling God's will.[3] Question submitted by the author: The Torah states, "Isaac said to Abraham, his father; he said, 'My father.'" Why does the Torah repeat the verb "[he] said" (which is one conjugated word in Hebrew)? It should have sufficed to say: Isaac said to Abraham, his father, "My father."

NL: *Perhaps here, too, we see doubt and fear, and Isaac hesitates as to whether or not he should ask his father this question.*[4]

B.   Questions and Analyses in Rashi

1(a)   Rashi asks why God uses multiple descriptions for the son to be taken for an offering and does not simply say, "Take Isaac." (NL: ג – correct)

---

3   There is great merit to this resolution proposed by Nechama Leibowitz. The proof text I offered from Genesis 27:32 is not typical biblical form and, therefore, may not be a solid support to my suggestion. As noted in this book's chapter "Inner Thoughts Revealed," an elongated introduction describing Isaac may well be reflecting Isaac's hesitation or confusion. The inclusion, in verse 32, of the reference to אָבִיו, "his father," may be indicating that while confused by the unfolding events, Isaac, nevertheless, recognized his second visitor as one of his sons; however, as we learn from the continuation of the verse, he was not confident as to which son stood before him.

It should also be noted that while delayed, Abraham does include the reference of בְּנִי, "my son," in his response to Isaac. Its position, being separated from Abraham's name, may be indicating – as Nechama suggested – that Abraham is focusing on his obligation to God, which he must make primary relative to his relationship with his son. Alternatively, by delaying the reference to "my son," the Torah may be sharing with us that Abraham tried to respond as quickly as possible to Isaac, who was troubled by the situation. While the inclusion of the name Abraham (as opposed to just וַיֹּאמֶר, "*he* said") does extend the introduction, it is necessary to alert us that Abraham needed to bring the strength of his personality to meet this challenge. Having done so, he turns his attention as quickly as possible to Isaac to try to allay *his* anxiety.

4   This hesitation is conveyed by elongating the introductory phrase and also by including the additional statement, "He said, 'My father.'" The verse could have reduced the introduction to only "Isaac said." Although the additional words may be seen as not adding any details to the actual events of the story, they definitely heighten the story's drama.

(b) In order to answer this question, we must understand the meaning of the phrase quoted by Rashi "to endear upon him the command." Does it mean to make Abraham feel more endearment towards fulfillment of the command? If so, why should Abraham's reward be increased? The easier it is for him to perform the command, the less reward he should receive!

Alternatively, one may understand the phrase to indicate that Abraham's fulfillment of the command was made more cherished. God expressed the command in a manner that prevented Abraham from becoming startled and confused and yet, upon reflection, also highlighted the many ways in which Isaac was special to Abraham. God thereby made it more difficult for Abraham to fulfill the command. When Abraham nevertheless prepared to fulfill it, his action was very dear to God. I am inclined to favor the latter explanation of "to make the command dear to him."[5] (NL: I too.)

According to this explanation, we can learn that God did not want Abraham to fulfill the commandment without a complete understanding of the consequences of his actions. Had Abraham been shocked by the command and fulfilled it in a compromised mental state, his actions would not have been as cherished or as valuable as a message to the world. Abraham's readiness to fulfill God's command serves as a model for us, today and in all generations. We must fulfill the Torah's commandments even when they are difficult for us and even when we have reason to ignore them. (NL: טב – "Very good")

The commentary of the Be'er Isaac, referenced in question B1b, seems to suggest the following contradiction: How could Abraham receive a reward for each and every one of God's statements if Abraham did not know to whom God was referring, since Isaac's name is not specified until late in the command? His primary answer to this question is that each Divine utterance provided another hint that prompted Abraham to consider that God was referring to Isaac.

---

5 This interpretation is similar to one offered by the Levush ha-Ora, a commentator on Rashi whose work is included in *Otzar Perushim*. The Levush ha-Ora suggests that "to endear upon him the command" should be understood as "to make dear to him the son that God termed as the singular one, the one who is beloved."

2. Here [the command to sacrifice Isaac], the demand on Abraham is enormous. Abraham's entire nature stands in opposition to this type of action. Therefore, it must be emphasized that he still moved briskly to fulfill the command and did not procrastinate. The demand to expel Ishmael was not as challenging. (NL)

3(a) Rashi questions the use of the word כֹּה; its usual meaning is "so" or "like this" (e.g. "so says The Lord," כֹּה אָמַר ה') and not "farther."

(b) Since there are other Hebrew words which could have conveyed the literal meaning of Abraham's statement (e.g. we will go עַד שָׁם, up to there, or עַד הַמָּקוֹם הַהוּא, up to that place), Rashi understands the Torah's use of the word כֹּה in a seemingly strange context as a hint of Abraham's inner thoughts. These thoughts are communicated by the Midrash Aggadah.[6] (NL)

(c) The Midrash represents Abraham's internal struggle. He is committed to fulfilling the Divine command but does not understand it. It seems to stand in conflict with God's promise כֹּה יִהְיֶה זַרְעֶךָ "[like the stars] so shall be your offspring." (NL טמ – "Very good")

---

6 In discussing the use of כֹּה, Nechama Leibowitz referenced a similar question from Exodus 7:16:

וְאָמַרְתָּ אֵלָיו יְהוָה אֱלֹהֵי הָעִבְרִים שְׁלָחַנִי אֵלֶיךָ לֵאמֹר שַׁלַּח אֶת־עַמִּי וְיַעַבְדֻנִי בַּמִּדְבָּר וְהִנֵּה לֹא־שָׁמַעְתָּ עַד־כֹּה׃

You shall say to him, "The Lord of the Hebrews sent me to you saying, 'Let My nation go and worship Me in the desert,' and behold, you have not listened until כֹּה (now)."

Rashi cites a midrashic interpretation: "Until you hear from me the Plague of the Firstborn, which I will begin with the words כֹּה אָמַר ה' כַּחֲצֹת הַלַּיְלָה – 'so said God: About midnight.'" Nechama explained that כֹּה is not a word usually used to communicate time. When God told Moses what to say to Pharaoh, God should have said, "עַד עַתָּה – until now" or "עַד הַיּוֹם until today." The Midrash and Rashi inform us that the use of the word כֹּה in an unusual fashion conveys a message that goes beyond a surface understanding of the verse.

ג ל י ו נ ו ת ל ע י ו ן ב פ ר ש ת ה ש ב ו ע

ערוכים בידי נחמה ליבוביץ   שנת ה'ארבע עשרה

יוצא לאור ע"י מוסד תורה והשכלה לכבוגרים ולנוער
הסתדרות נשי מזרחי. באמריקה

מהדורה מיוחדת בסביל האסתדרות הציונית העולמית
- המחלקה לחנוך ולתרבות תורניים בגולה

וירא (תשט"ו)   פרק כ"ב העקדה

חמש גליון וירא תט"ז שעסק כולו במוטב ה"נסיון" בפסוק א' "וחאלוקים
נסה את אברהם".

א. סאלות מבנה וסגנון

1) תשובח אברהם בפסוק א' באה בין שתי אטירות של חאלוקים, ואין תשובה
מצד אברהם אבינו באה לאחר האטירה השניה של האלוקים.

הסבר מדוע?

2) השיחת סבין אברהם ויצחק - היחידה בפרק, בפסוקים ז - ח - באה בין
סני חצאי פסוקים טוים, בין סתי הפעטים של "וילכו סניהם יחדו".

מה מטמעותח של חזרת זו ומדוע העמדו טלים אלה במקום זה דוקא
לפני ולאחרי הכיחת?

3) טים לב לפרס קטן בסטימה ביין אברהם ויצחק:

ז.. ויאמר	: אבי
ויאמר	: חננ'י, בני
ויאמר	: הנה האש והעצים. ואית הסה לעולה?
ויאמר אברהם	: אלוחים יראה לו. הסה לעולה בני.

התוכל למצוא את הסבה למה הוסיף הכתוב בסוף את הסם "אברהם",
סלא כדרך סגנון התורה?
העזר בגליון תולדות חמ"י סאלה ב.

ב. סאלות ודיוקים ברס"י:

1) א ד"ה את בנך: אמר לו: "סני	(א) מה קסה לו בפסקונו?
בנים יס לי", אמר לו: .."את	
יחידך". אמר לו: "זה יחיד לאטו	(ב)× בעל באר יצחק על רס"י. מעיר
וזה יחיד לאמו". אמר לו: "אסר	סרס"י נותן כאן סתי תשובות
אהבת". אמר לו: "סניחם אני	מנוגדות ליסב קוטיתו,
אוהב". אמר לו: "את יצחק" -	הסבר מה חנגוד גביניחן וכיצד
ולמה לא גלה לו מתחלה? סלא	יתקימו זו בצד זו.
לערבבו פתאום ותזוח דעתו עליו	
ותטרף וכדי לחבב עליו את המצוה	וע' גם ברטב"ן ד"ה קח נא את
ולידתן לו סכר על כל דבור ודבור.	בנך.

2) ג ד"ה ויטכם:	(א)(ב) הסוה לדבריו כאן דברי רד"ק כ"א
	י"ד ד"ה ויטכם; "לקיים מצוה האל".
	התוכל להסביר למה אין רס"י אומר
	דבריו סאמר לפסוקנו גם לפטוק
	ההוא - כפי סעסה רד"ק?

3) ח ד"ה עד כה:	(א) מה קסה לו? !
כלומר: דרך מועט למקום	
אסר לפניגו.ומדרש אגדה:	(ב)× מדוע לא הסהפק רט"י כאן בפר יס
אמר: "אראה"- היכן הוא	כפטוטו והוסיף עליו עוד מדרס
מה שאמר לי המקום:	אגדה?
"כה יהיה זרעך".	וע' רס"י כמות ז' ט"ז והנה
	לא סמעת ע': כח.

	(ג) הסבר מה הרעיון חמסוטל בדברי
	הפדרס חזה?
	(והסות למדרס מסוג זח:
	טדרס אבכיר סמות ב י"ב "ויפן
	כה וכה" אמר מטה לפניו: רבונו

A Letter from Nechama Leibowitz

Frequently, during the many years in which my primary communication with Nechama Leibowitz was through the written word, Nechama would conclude her responses inquiring, "When will you return to visit?" or, "When will you come to live in Israel?" The letter translated below was addressed to me during my tenure as rabbi of Congregation Beth Tefillah, Paramus, New Jersey.

Purim 5751/1991

Dear Benjamin

I thank you for writing to me about your activities and the holy work with which you are involved. I have only to bless you that you will continue to perform and succeed.

It appears to me that the work of a congregational rabbi in the Diaspora must be in its essence to influence the *generation of youth* that it should be loathsome to them to live in the Diaspora, dependent upon the gentiles, after nearly 2000 years, at a time that they have a state *of their own*, which they merited through the kindness of G-d, already more than 40 years ago. They should come and live in it and *help to build it* and participate in this *noble and wondrous* enterprise. Is it the task of a healthy, smart, intelligent Jewish youth *at this time* to promote the growth and blossoming of the United States, to give of his strength and energy and wisdom a gift *to the states of the Diaspora*??! Are there not approximately 220 million people living in the United States? *They will do fine without the Jewish youth* ([be they] a doctor or an engineer or an instructor or a secretary or a kindergarten teacher or an official or . . . or . . .). If only they would come *to us*; each Jew who comes to us is needed by us; we're *lacking*; everyone is a stone in the noble structure which is our obligation to establish.

If you will see *your task **in this vein***, to show them that their residence there is essentially an embarrassment to us and a lack of appreciation to the Holy One blessed be He, Who performed for us miracles and wonders these entire 40 years and *enables* us to remove from ourselves the shame of the Diaspora – if you will see *this* as your task, then there is *great reason* in your dwelling there.

I have another letter from you but the workload which is upon me is very great. I corrected what I corrected and I seized the opportunity of this Purim vacation for this [i.e., some of the answers submitted]. And the rest will be at another time.

And peace, peace to you and all that is yours,

Nechama

פורים תשנ"א

בנימין היקר

אני מודה לך שכתבת לי על מעשיך ועבודת הקדש שאתה עסוק בה. ויש לי רק לברכך עשה והצלח.

נדמה לי שעבודת רב בקהילה בגולה צריכה בעיקר להיות להשפיע על <u>הדור הצעיר</u> שימְאַס עליהם לשבת בגולה, סמוכים על שולחן הגוים – אחרי קרוב ל-2000 שנה, בשעה שיש להם מדינה <u>משלהם</u>, שזכו לה בחסדי ה' וכבר למעלה מ-40 שנה, ויבואו ויתישבו בה <u>ויעזרו לבנותה</u> וישתתפו במפעל <u>האדיר והנפלא הזה</u>. האם זהו תפקידו של צעיר בריא חכם אינטליגנטי יהודי <u>בשעה זו</u> להגדיל ולהפְרִיח את ארצות הברית, לתת מִכּחֹו וּמֶרְצוֹ וּמֵחָכְמתוֹ תרומה <u>לארצות הגולה</u>??! הלא בארצות הברית יושבים כ-220 מליון נפש, הם <u>יסתדרו גם בלי הצעיר היהודי הזה</u> (רופא או מהנדס או מורה או מזכירה, או גננת או פקיד או... או...) ואלו <u>לנו</u> כל יהודי הבא אלינו דרוש לנו, <u>חסר</u> לנו, כל אחד הוא אבן בבנין האדיר שעלינו להקימו.

ואם תראה את <u>תפקידך בזה</u> להראות להם, שכל ישיבתם שם היא בעצם בושה לנו וחוסֶר הַכָּרת תודה לקב"ה שעשה עמנו נסים ונפלאות כל 40 שנה אלה <u>ומאפשר</u> לנו להסיר מעלינו את חרפת הגולה – אם תראה <u>בזה</u> את תפקידך, הרי יש <u>טעם רב</u> בשבתך שם.

יש לי עוד מכתב ממך אבל העבודה המוטלת עלי רבה מאד ותקנתי מה שתקנתי וניצַלְתי את חפש פורים לזה. והשְׁאָר בפעם אחרת.

ושלום שלום לך ולכל אשר לך

נחמה.

Transcription of letter

ברוך השם

בנימין היקר

אני מודה לך [illegible]

[illegible]

[illegible]

[illegible]

הבלים - אחרי קרוב ל2000 שנה, [illegible]

[illegible]

[illegible]

הסביר [illegible] האם [illegible]

[illegible]

[illegible]

[illegible] 220 מליון נפש,

הם יסתדרו גם בלי [illegible] היהודי [illegible]

או [illegible] או [illegible], או [illegible] או פקיד או [illegible]

[illegible]

[illegible]

[illegible]

[illegible]

[illegible]

[illegible]

[illegible]

[illegible]

[illegible]

[illegible]

[illegible]

[illegible]

Photocopy of original letter